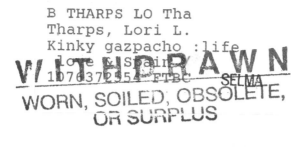

kinky gazpacho

lori l. tharps

kinky
gazpacho

life, love & spain

ATRIA BOOKS

NEW YORK   LONDON   TORONTO   SYDNEY

ATRIA BOOKS
A Division of Simon & Schuster, Inc.
1230 Avenue of the Americas
New York, NY 10020

First Atria Books hardcover edition March 2008

ATRIA BOOKS and colophon are trademarks of Simon & Schuster, Inc.

For information about special discounts for bulk purchases, please contact Simon & Schuster Special Sales at 1-800-456-6798 or business@ simonandschuster.com.

Designed by Karolina Harris

Manufactured in the United States of America

10 9 8 7 6 5 4 3 2 1

Library of Congress Cataloging-in-Publication Data
Tharps, Lori L.
   Kinky gazpacho : life, love & Spain / Lori L. Tharps.
p. cm.
1. Tharps, Lori L. 2. Tharps, Lori L.—Travel—Spain. 3. Spain—Description and travel. 4. Spain—Civilization. 5. Milwaukee (Wisc.)—Biography. 6. Multicultural education—Wisconsin—Milwaukee. 7. African American students—Spain—Biography. 8. African American women—Spain—Biography. 9. American students—Spain—Biography. 10. Americans—Spain—Biography. I. Title.
DP48.T48 2007
946.083092—dc22
[B]   2007006424

ISBN-13: 978-0-7432-9647-2
ISBN-10:   0-7432-9647-8

Para Manuel. Of course.

Contents

Author's Note

This is a memoir. The story told is true the way I remember it. However, many names and identifying details have been changed to protect the innocent people who have passed through my life and never volunteered to have their lives exposed. Some time sequences have also been altered to keep the story going forward. But for the most part, I begin at the beginning and end at the end.

kinky gazpacho

✻ 1 : International Day

Milwaukee, Wisconsin. 1980.

Third grade.

Right before dismissal.

We were sitting on the rug at the end of the day listening to Mrs. Fletcher explain about International Day. It was going to be something new and exciting and we were all going to participate. The gymnasium would be transformed into an international bazaar and there was going to be food and games and decorations from all over the world. I looked around at my classmates to see if anyone else thought this sounded exciting. Blank stares all around. Mrs. Fletcher continued, undeterred by our collective lack of enthusiasm. "So regular classes will be suspended for the entire day . . . ," she started, and then of course everyone perked up. "And we will spend the afternoon at the bazaar learning about different cultures. And the best part is you don't have to wear your uniforms." Some of the kids whooped and hollered at that. I didn't really care. I actually liked my Black Watch plaid jumper with the gold buttons on the shoulders. It made me feel official. And my regular play clothes were not that cute anyway, thanks to having a mom who swore she could find the same designer clothing at the JCPenney warehouse that the other kids got from the Polo store and Laura Ashley.

Still, this bazaar thing had potential. I liked learning about different cultures and *anything* involving food and eating made me happy. My best friend was Japanese and I had already discovered a great love of tofu drenched in soy sauce. And thin, salty, crispy strips of seaweed made an excellent snack food. Thanks to Miko, I even knew how to say "grandma," "grandpa," and "soy sauce" in Japanese. And I could eat rice with chopsticks. Nobody else in my class could do that. I was about to raise my hand and offer up this bit of information to Mrs. Fletcher and the rest of my classmates when I remembered that Mrs. Fletcher had recently commented to my parents that I asked too many questions in class and needed to exercise some self-control. My mother, believing there was no such thing as too many questions, suggested I simply wait until the teacher was done talking before I shot my hand up in the air. "Just don't interrupt her so much," is what my mother told me, so I willed my hand still and waited for her to finish her instructions so I could share my wealth of information about Japanese culture.

"So," Mrs. Fletcher was saying, "instead of your uniforms you are all supposed to come to school dressed in the clothing of your ancestors. So if your family is German you can wear lederhosen or one of those cute dresses with the white pinafore." This being Milwaukee, the majority of my white classmates claimed German heritage and got it right away. Melissa Konig raised her hand, a look of concern wrinkling her lightly freckled face. "What if you're German on one side and French on the other?" she asked. Mrs. Fletcher laughed. "You can pick whichever part of your heritage you want to display." Another kid raised his hand. "What if we don't know our heritage?" Again laughter from the teacher. "Your parents know exactly where they came from," she assured us. "And that's part of the reason for this day. We want you to investigate where you come from and share it with the school community. You can bring in decorations or foods or pictures or anything. The entire lower school will be involved."

Suddenly Japanese culture wasn't important anymore. I felt my cheeks burn. If they hadn't been brown, everyone would have noticed that they were red. I tried not to make eye contact with anyone, in case they noticed my discomfort or figured out my shame. My ancestors were slaves! I was the descendant of a group of people kept as chattel, who lived in shacks, worked themselves to death, and, if luck was on their side, fled up north with Harriet Tubman and disappeared. What was I supposed to do? Come to school dressed in rags with a handkerchief tied around my head? And food? Slaves didn't get to eat good food. Maybe my mom could bring in some table scraps for everyone to sample. I could feel my heart beating loudly in my chest and my skin went cold. How was I going to deal with this? And me being the only Black child in my class, my shame was my own.

"Are there any other questions?" Mrs. Fletcher asked, looking directly at me. I quickly averted my gaze and shook my head no. I didn't want her to bring up my predicament in front of everyone. Maybe she'd tell me I didn't have to come to school on Friday, seeing as I didn't have a "real" heritage like everyone else. Luckily the boys in my class, unable to sit still any longer, freed me from my dilemma by jumping up and heading to the coatroom, effectively ending the discussion.

I dragged myself out the door and to the front circle to wait for the school bus. The ride to our house in Shorewood, a suburb of Milwaukee that felt like city living with more trees, lasted an hour. Usually Vivian Cole and I sat in the very back seats and sang classic rock songs at the top of our lungs to pass the time, but this day, I sat alone in an anonymous middle seat and tried not to cry. Life was so unfair. It had never really bothered me before that I was the only Black girl in my class and one of only a handful in my entire private school. In fact, I barely even noticed. And as far as I could tell, nobody else noticed, either. Nobody ever referred to me as "that Black girl" or called me names. I was just Lori. Now everyone was going to know I was different. They'd realize my history made me something less than they were. I went from sad to angry. By the time Vince the bus driver called me out of my funk to let me know I was home, I felt royally cheated that I wasn't from a legitimate country like Germany or England. Or someplace exotic like Greece, which is where Kristopher Stavros was from. For every birthday since the first grade, Kristopher's mother had brought in homemade sticky-sweet baklava, which, she was always careful to explain in her heavily accented English, took hours to make. But little Kristopher was worth it. Which I always questioned, since in class little Kristopher was a major pain in the butt, but that's not really important.

"What's the matter with you?" my mother asked when I came shuffling through the front door. She was always home to get me off the bus, having worked the early shift at the hospital. I told her about International Day and my embarrassing predicament.

"Oh, don't be so dramatic," she said, pooh-poohing my self-inflicted trauma. "You can wear whatever you want. In fact, you can wear my red beret, and I saw this perfect blue dress the other day that looks just like Madeline's from the book. You can be French," my mother said.

"But we're not French," I squeaked, wanting to believe my mother had the right idea, imagining myself in an adorable French outfit to rival Melissa Konig's. And I did look good in a beret. I'd tried on my mother's when she was taking a nap.

"We might be," my mother said. "I've always felt very drawn to French culture," she added.

But this wasn't ethnic Halloween. I could just imagine showing up at school all Frenchied up and then having to explain to people how a Black person could possibly be French. We'd all seen the same history books, and not once did I ever recall a single Black person in France. People would just laugh at me—or worse, call me a liar.

"Forget it," I said to my mother. "I just won't wear anything. I'll just say we couldn't find anything."

"Lori, you're being silly," my mother tried again. "You could wear something Dutch. I know for sure that on your father's side someone was Dutch. We could find some wooden clogs and—"

"Mom, Dutch people have blond hair and blue eyes. Like that boy on the paint can," I interrupted. "Who is going to believe me when I say I'm Dutch?"

"Well you *are* partially Dutch," my mother sniffed. This conversation was making her uncomfortable, which was making me uncomfortable. I wanted a solution from her that not only made sense, but would also put me back on equal footing with my friends. I wanted to wear a costume like everyone else and be like everyone else, but in this instance I couldn't. And I couldn't bear the thought of wearing an outfit that belonged to the slave-owning part of my heritage and then having to explain how we were connected. I didn't feel as if I had permission to claim the master's culture. It wasn't ours for the taking. And I certainly wasn't going to explain all this to the kids at my school on International Day.

My mother gave it one last effort. "Would you prefer to go dressed as an Indian? I know for a fact that my grandmother on my mother's side was half Cherokee Indian."

I left the room without answering.

It was true that my mother's people had some real Native American blood in them. But who didn't? My mother was born in Egypt, Mississippi, one of ten girls and one boy. Her family moved to Milwaukee when she was four and she never left, except for the two years in Cincinnati while my father got his MBA at Xavier University. On my dad's side of the family, everyone always talked about an Indian relative on my grandmother's side that was responsible for their high yellow skin color and almost indigo eyes. Like my dad's. But no one had ever been able to tell me much about this phantom relative whenever I pressed for details. In fact, they couldn't even confirm whether he was an Indian from India or a Native American.

As I lay across my bed, racking my brain trying to come up with some exotic element in my family tree, I realized how very little I actually did know. My mother's family seemed to start and stop with my aunties and cousins. They were my family, my history, and my ancestors. Each auntie had her own "thing" that made her special. Mary was the cook. Minerva was the beauty expert. Linda Sue, the baby of the girls still living in Milwaukee, was the one you went to for laughs. I thought I had parts of them all in my body. My dad's family all lived in Baltimore and we only saw them on holidays and sometimes in the summer. I never even bothered to ask my grandmother anything about where she came from. I figured if we descended from something special, then I'd have heard about it by now. I fell asleep on my bed dreaming of slave shacks and Harriet Tubman.

On Friday morning I put my uniform on. I considered pretending to be sick, but my parents didn't allow that. My father had actually divided our tuition by the hours we were in school to calculate how much each class was worth, so he could say things like "If you miss an entire day of school, that's thirty dollars down the drain. One class, you're talking five bucks." Plus, as uncomfortable as I was, I was still really interested in tasting all that international food. Miko's family had recently taken my sister and me to a real German restaurant in Chicago and made us try snails dripping with butter and garlic. I was hoping that with all the Germans in my school, there'd be some of those at International Day.

When I got to school, all the kids in my class were wearing the expected lederhosen and cutesy pinafore dresses, berets, and knickers, and one kid had on a pair of wooden shoes. The one Indian boy in my class, Vikas, wore something made of silk that looked like a dress and had a funny name. Mrs. Fletcher didn't even ask me where my costume was. She probably assumed I wouldn't want to come dressed like a slave. I was relieved she didn't ask me to explain myself.

The activities started at lunchtime. Our usual family-style meal was a smorgasbord of international flavors. We had bratwurst and apple turnovers, Swedish meatballs and some sort of Chinese stir-fry with crunchy noodles. No snails, though. After lunch we headed to the gym and were met with a riot of color and noise and information. We went around as a class first, visiting the different booths. Each booth represented a different country and was manned by volunteer parents in costumes. And then we were free to roam around, playing games, sampling sweets, and reading about distant lands. As I meandered around the gym, I completely forgot about my lack of heritage and just enjoyed all the activities with my friends. And then it was time for the parade of costumes, and I moved to the edge of the floor. I wasn't the only one without a costume, though. Other kids had forgotten or couldn't find anything to wear. I tried to act like I belonged with them.

By the time International Day was over, I felt like I had been holding my breath and I could finally let it go. All day long I had been praying nobody would ask me where I came from and why I wasn't wearing a costume. The fact that they didn't ask made me realize that they all probably knew and didn't want to make me feel bad. Everybody knew that Black people came from nothing.

2: Josephine Baker Was My Hero

"Mom," I hollered, hoping she could hear me all the way downstairs, "I have to decide between Spanish and French. Which should I take?"

I didn't hear a response. My mother probably wasn't answering because she hated when I tried to carry on conversations between different parts of the house. It didn't matter. I pretty much knew what language she would choose. French. Even though she herself had studied equal years of Spanish and French in high school and college, she claimed she knew French better. It was a cultured language and very useful in many different countries and for ballet and music, too. My older sister, Elisa, agreed with my mother's philosophy and had opted for French three years earlier when she entered the fifth grade. The fact that she was an aspiring ballerina weighed in on her decision as well.

As I pored over the packet of information I had received from the school about fifth grade, which was the official beginning of middle school, I started getting really excited. Besides the fact that I could retire my babyish jumper for a uniform skirt, middle school meant changing classes for math, science, and language. It meant study halls and lockers instead of a coat hook. It meant Dunkin' Donuts for sale in the lobby every Thursday morning. It meant my sister and I (Elisa was heading to the eighth grade) would pass each other in the halls. I'd get total cool points for being acknowledged by all of my sister's older friends. But as much as I worshiped Elisa, I also knew the necessity of distinguishing myself from her. It had already been established that Elisa was the good student. The dutiful, hardworking, good-grade-getting type. Teachers loved her. Me? I asked too many questions, talked too much, and didn't have the discipline to study hard enough to excel. So in order to diminish the inevitable comparisons, I checked the box next to Spanish to spare myself and others the "You're not what I expected from Elisa's sister" comments.

I announced my intention to study Spanish at the dinner table that night. I didn't explain my decision-making process.

"I think Spanish is a good idea," my father said. "Hispanics are the fastest-growing minority and you're going to need to speak Spanish to get ahead in any business."

"Um, Dad, I'm not even interested in business," I said, wondering if my dad had any clue what the life of a ten-year-old was even about. He was an accountant, so probably not.

"Are you sure you don't want to study French?" my mother tried one more time.

"Yeah, I'm sure," I said. "I mean, Elisa's already taking French, so I should probably take Spanish so our family is like representing all the languages," I said, hoping that sounded legitimate.

"Well, you'll have Mr. Betancourt for a teacher," my sister chimed in. "He's really nice. I had him last year. Everyone calls him Mr. B."

My heart sank. "What do you mean you had him? Isn't he the Spanish teacher?" I asked, hoping against hope that my sister was merely confused.

"Yeah, but he teaches one class of French, too. He's Cuban and supposedly something horrible happened to his family in Cuba but you're not supposed to talk about it."

I was intrigued. But mostly I was bummed because now I had to disappoint yet another educator at the University School of Milwaukee.

Mr. Betancourt wore a lot of cologne. Like a lot a lot. His classroom reeked of the sweet, musky scent. And it oozed from his pores. I imagined that he even splashed some on his always-shiny mane of dyed black hair. But then again, everything about Mr. B. was bold and over the top. He dressed like none of the other male teachers at my school. No gray pants and blue blazers. Mr. B. liked color. Lots of color. Red-and-white checkered pants, hot pink dress shirts. Bow ties and shiny white patent leather shoes. I liked him right away. And despite the fact that he'd had the pleasure of instructing my sister first, he liked me, too.

"Okay." Mr. B. was trying again to inspire us. He held up the large picture of a cartoon family relaxing in the living room. He pointed to the lamp in the picture.

"*¿Esto qué es?*" he asked. Someone shouted out, "*Lámpara.*" Mr. B.'s head fell into his hands. Apparently we were hopeless. His face turned red as he tried to maintain some semblance of control. He willed his thin lips into a smile, showing just enough teeth for it to be misconstrued as a snarl. With his index finger, he again pointed to the lamp and asked, "*¿Esto qué es?*"

I knew what he wanted.

I raised my hand. "*Esto es una lámpara.*" Full sentences, people.

I got a "*muy bien*" and a grateful smile. He moved on to the couch. "*¿Esto qué es?*" I couldn't help myself and raised my hand again. Shamelessly, Mr. B. called on me again because he knew I wouldn't disappoint him. "*Esto es un sofá.*" I'm not that talented with languages, but come on, "*lámpara*" and "*sofá*" sound the same in English. It wasn't that hard. Still, a lot of my classmates just heard "foreign language" and their brains immediately shut down. Not me. Learning Spanish had opened my eyes to a world beyond Milwaukee, where I had spent my entire decade of life. Granted, we moved like clockwork every two years, but we always stayed firmly planted on the North Shore of Milwaukee, where we also always managed to integrate a new neighborhood.

In Spanish class we were all foreigners, learning a new language and a new culture. Nobody entered that room with any type of hometown advantage. Having the last name Bradley or Uihlien wouldn't help you roll your r's or conjugate the subjunctive. I secretly thought Mr. B. liked me a little better because my brown skin might have re-

minded him of Cuba. Maybe his missing wife was Black and I reminded him of his daughter. Granted, I didn't even know if he had a
daughter, but I had no problem standing in if he needed a surrogate.
I was always looking for a good role to play.

After one year of Spanish it was all over. My parents decided to send
my sister and me to public school, and they didn't teach Spanish in
public school in the sixth grade.

"We're not moving anymore, so you guys can go to the neighborhood schools," my parents announced over the summer. "The schools
in Shorewood are really good, and with the money we're paying in
taxes to live here we ought to get the benefit of sending you guys to
public school," my father explained to us.

But I knew the real reason we were being exiled to public school.
My parents had run out of money. The giant abandoned mansion
they had bought as the granddaddy of all their crazy house-restoration
projects had rapidly depleted their resources. As had the unexpected
birth of my little brother in 1980. We were broke. The way my parents
were always arguing over money, I feared one day my father would
be sent to jail for not paying a bill. Even the cars my parents were
driving proved that we were two steps away from skid row. We'd been
downgraded from a respectable secondhand Mercedes and a sensible
1970s station wagon my sister had named Goldie to what we called
the Sherman Tank. It was a sand-colored gargantuan heap of ugly that
was so big and so tacky, Elisa and I hid on the floor of the backseat
when we were forced to ride in it. It even smelled like ugly.

I cried and protested the decision, but to no avail. I'd never be
able to look my University School friends in the eye ever again with
this public-school shame. Luckily, they all lived in the suburbs close
to school, so the likelihood of bumping into them was small. Still,
I cringed at just the thought of explaining to Diane or Sally why I
wouldn't be back at USM in the fall. My mother tried to help me see
the positive side of things.

"You'll be able to walk to school instead of riding that silly bus for
an hour," she said.

"I like riding the bus," I responded, which was entirely true be-cause Vivian and I often convinced Vince to stop at Baskin-Robbins for ice cream before dropping us off.

"You'll be able to make friends in the neighborhood," she offered. To her credit, I did routinely complain about all my friends living so far away that I never got to just go over to their houses. It always had to be prearranged with somebody's parent playing chauffeur. What I had hoped to accomplish with my constant complaints was that we would move closer to them. Not me making new friends closer to home.

Luckily, the public-school experiment was a colossal failure. My sister, a freshman at the high school, immediately fell in with a fast crowd of party animals who kept her away from the house and her books for long periods of unexplained time. Yet she managed to pull off straight A's and even get exempt from several exams because of her high marks in class. This didn't sound right to my parents. And I, too, had found the academic standards in my sixth-grade class to be woefully below what I had experienced the year before. Academically I yawned through sixth grade and was at the head of the class. Socially, however, I had a lot to learn.

My first lesson came from a Black girl named Tanya Montgomery. Tanya was my best friend for the first three weeks of school. Then one day she hated me. She started a coatroom smear campaign against me, telling anyone who would listen that I was a liar and had been openly criticizing Amy Taylor's purple ruffled shirt. Yes, it was true, I had mentioned something about the shirt reminding me of a certain elflike character on a popular television show, but that was told in confidence to another girl. Tanya had no business announcing this to the class as a symbol of my inherent evilness. By the end of the week, rumors were circulating that Tanya planned to "get me good" as soon as she could on the playground.

From what I could gather, Tanya had been the Everybody Knows and Likes Her Black Girl in the school before me. There were three Black girls in our grade altogether before I showed up, all of them bused in from the city. They were all friends, but Tanya was the ringleader. She was the voice. Well, my loud mouth and effervescent personality apparently rattled Tanya's lock on the sixth-grade Black-girl popularity contest. Apparently there was room for only one Black girl queen bee. Or so she thought. And she planned on showing me who reigned supreme. Of course, back at private school, playground politics never got this gritty, so I just assumed Tanya was a crazy girl. And so I hid from her. Constantly. I avoided being alone at recess time. Walked home every day for lunch to avoid her in the cafeteria. Never returned to the school grounds until precisely one minute before the school bell rang. One day I miscalculated my timing and arrived back at school with a good five minutes of recess still left. She was waiting for me and immediately got in my face.

"Why don't you go back to where you came from?" she said to me, pushing me for emphasis.

I wanted a nasty comeback to burst forth from my mouth, but instead "Why don't you?" came weakly from my lips. And I shoved her back.

And then she pushed me and I fell in the dirt and suddenly our classmates, eager for entertainment and ready for blood, surrounded us. Tears were already running down my cheeks as I braced myself for the next attack. But it never came. The teacher did instead. She pulled us apart and told us both to go inside. I was so grateful I ran to the bathroom to clean myself up. One of the other Black girls followed me in. I feared for my life.

As I acted like cleaning my face was the most important job in the world, Tiffany came up to me and asked me a question.

"Is your daddy White?" she asked me.

"No. Why?" I responded.

"Well, why do you talk like that?"

"Like what?" I asked, even though I knew what she meant. Almost every Black person in Milwaukee had accused me of talking White.

"Well, you should just stay out of Tanya's way," she advised. "She'll leave you alone. You just bother her, acting all uppity and stuff."

"Okay," I said, grateful that she wasn't here to beat me up, but wondering how I was supposed to stop acting uppity when I wasn't acting. I was just being. But now I understood that it wasn't the purple shirt and I wasn't a liar. This Black girl wanted to beat my ass because I wasn't acting like a real Black person was supposed to. She just wanted me to act right, instead of White.

What I did instead was spend the rest of the year avoiding the Black people at my new school and trying to repair my damaged reputation with the White kids, doing my best to convince them that except for my Black skin, I was just like them. And I kept my opinions about other people's taste in clothing to myself.

I don't how they did it, but money or no money, my parents realized their social experiment hadn't worked. One year later, my sister and I were promptly returned to our private school utopia.

Public school had changed me. Before sixth grade I thought life was all about the comings and goings of the inhabitants of River Hills, the tony suburb where University School reigned supreme. Now I knew the world had more to offer than this *Dynasty*-meets-the-Midwest experience. Some of it scared me, but I was intrigued by the possibilities other places might offer.

By the time I got reacquainted with my seventh-grade Spanish class, I began to obsess about traveling to Spain. With its bold and colorful history, filled with passion and romance, Spain seemed to be the perfect place for a girl with a penchant for drama to find herself. With very little research, I just decided Spain was going to be my salvation. I just felt it. I couldn't explain why, but I knew my future was somehow linked to the Iberian Peninsula. I wrote in my diary one day, "Spain is going to change my life," and believed in it forever. Something about the way I felt in Spanish class made me feel so good about myself and my own potential. Mr. Betancourt was still my teacher and loved to fuel my fantasies of Spanish living. I took everything he taught me so seriously. From the great Spanish painters to his recipe for custardy sweet flan, I absorbed everything like a sponge. I felt like I was taking notes for my future. I wasn't just studying Spanish because I had to learn a language; I wanted access into another world when this one got to be too much.

It only made sense that he was going to ask me. He pulled me into his classroom after school one day. "Lori," he said in his husky English, "come let me show you the pictures from Spain." Every year during spring break, Mr. Betancourt led a group of eighth graders to Spain. Next year I would be eligible to go, but I knew I wouldn't be on that plane. My parents, already struggling to pay the tuition for my sister, me, and now my little brother, Lee, would never pay two thousand dollars for me to be a tourist in Spain with my rich friends.

So I stood by Mr. Betancourt's desk trying to muster up some enthusiasm for seeing something I knew I would never experience. I dutifully oohed and ahhed over the group shots of this year's eighth graders standing in front of monuments and in parks looking bored and uninterested. I threw out some "*muy buenos*" and "*qué interesantes*" to try to show I cared, but the truth was I didn't. Even though I knew Spain was waiting to embrace me, I had no interest in this version. I wanted to live in Spain, not just visit. This touristy, prearranged, chaperoned Spain didn't inspire me. When I went to Spain, I was going to sit in cafés and restaurants and eat and drink the culture. I wanted to sample paella and stomp my feet to flamenco rhythms. I was going to speak with the people in their own language. I would walk the streets and people would recognize my greatness. I would not go with a group of Americans who would remind me where I came from.

It's not that I didn't like where I came from specifically. Milwaukee was a nice city with nice amenities, like big parks, the beach, and lots of ice-skating rinks. But it was boring and dull and colorless. So far in my twelve years, I'd seen only two types of people in Milwaukee, Black ones and White ones. There were a few Mexicans and Asians sprinkled here and there, but they were hard to spot. I dreamed in Technicolor. I wanted to sing and dance and act and be fabulous. I craved energy and lights. I'd gone to Los Angeles for spring break with my mom and gotten a taste of what life could really be about. In L.A. they had palm trees and pink houses and beautiful people with brown skin. We went to the Esprit store and there were pictures on the walls of Black girls with wild kinky hair who looked like me. That's pretty much the life I wanted. I wanted to be free like the girl in the Esprit ad, arms out embracing life. I couldn't do that in Black and White Milwaukee. I needed to go far away to find what I was looking for.

And Spain was really far away. For me, Spain was going to be as fabulous as Josephine Baker's Paris. Josephine was my idol. I knew her life story by heart and realized we had so much in common. She was poor, Black, and penniless. I was middle-class, Black, and felt penniless on account of the fact that everyone I went to school with was rich. She was from St. Louis, which was only a stretch from my hometown of Milwaukee. She couldn't be a famous dancer in St. Louis because she was Black. I couldn't be the most popular girl at my school because I was Black. Where she escaped her racist midwestern roots and landed in France, I would do the same in Spain. I even wanted to adopt my own tribe of rainbow children and preside over a multilingual, multicultural, multitalented household. I was thinking like *The Sound of Music*, but in color! Except for the dying alone and penniless part, I wanted to model my life on Josephine's. (Oh, and I didn't want to dance around naked wearing a banana skirt, either.)

The party was at Gloria Dean's house. She was an eighth grader. She was supremely popular and that had nothing to do with the fact that her grandfather was the sole proprietor of an important farm equipment conglomerate and that she got dropped off at school in fancy cars that rivaled Princess Diana's. Or maybe it did. Whatever the reason, I couldn't believe that I had made the list of invitees for her thirteenth birthday party. She was an eighth grader and had invited me, a seventh grader with no fashion sense. Yes, I did have a bubbly personality and could talk to just about anyone, but I never expected to be invited into the inner sanctum of the older and more popular.

Even my mother was excited. She actually surprised me by buying me a real designer outfit for the party.

"You can't be going to this kind of party looking sloppy," she said by way of explanation. She had bypassed Penney's and had gone straight to the Esprit section at Marshall Field's. The quilted pants were olive green. The shirt was a warm chocolate brown with pink and white vertical pinstripes, and, instead of buttons, closed with that

1980s wonder product, Velcro. I wore a pink cashmere vest over the shirt, and for a finishing touch, neon-yellow socks.

My hair was newly relaxed and curled, held back with a single bar-rette. When I descended the steps into the Deans' basement, I was holding my breath in anticipation. I knew I looked good. Better than I ever had for any other social event, where my usual attire consisted of shapeless sweatsuits or earth-toned corduroys with plain sweaters. As soon as I hit the party floor, my friends all magically appeared to appraise my new outfit. I could tell they were impressed by the way their eyes widened in shock with just a glint of jealousy, or perhaps it was disappointment that they had no reason to feel smug at their inherent superiority.

"Wow, you look great," my best friend Sally said. "Yeah," chimed in Diane, both of whom still bested me because besides having the right outfits they had the right shoes, too. Tiny, black patent leather Capezio ballet flats adorned with rhinestones and no socks! I looked down at my own big feet in hard brown lace-ups that my mother still forced me to wear in hopes that I might still, at age twelve, correct my ridiculously flat and slightly pigeon-toed feet. She claimed my brogues were the height of fashion in London, but here in Gloria Dean's basement, I might as well have been wearing Tweety Bird slippers. They were just plain wrong. I experienced a sharp pang of disappointment, but then I looked around and saw boys and girls mingling together, a whole corner of the room set up with a four-foot-long submarine sandwich, punch, and chips, and the music was booming. This was a real party. The kind I'd always hear the other girls talking about in study halls on Monday mornings, and I, Lori Lynn Tharps, was here. I felt superior all over again and promptly forgot about my sensible shoes.

"I'm going to go look around," I shouted to Diane and Sally over the music. Without waiting for a response I made my way toward the food table. Even though submarine sandwiches were my favorite, I didn't dare eat a piece in case I dripped mayonnaise or tomato seeds on my new clothes. Or worse, I could get onion breath from the raw onions and ruin my chances at having my first kiss. Which made me realize, I hadn't seen Topher yet. He was the focus of my (and every other seventh-grade girl's) heartfelt attention. With his dark brown hair, clear blue eyes, and smattering of freckles across his nose, he was just so cute. And even though he spoke few words, when he did, it was usually something incredibly smart or sarcastically funny. My crush ran deep.

And there he was. I turned to the punch bowl to try to compose myself and to plan how I was going to strike up a conversation with Topher. He was in my Spanish class and we had pre-algebra together. In math class I consistently made a fool of myself because I was always a step behind the rest of the class, but I knew Topher liked me well enough. What I didn't know was if he'd want to be seen with me at a party. But then I remembered how good I looked in my new clothes and decided that Topher, like my friends, would be so overwhelmed by my beauty he'd ignore his guy friends and invite me into one of the quieter parts of the basement and declare his affections and ask me to go steady with him. Buoyed by my fantasy and my confidence in the transforming powers of Esprit, I headed over to the group of boys. Topher saw me, and his thin, pink lips curled into a smile. I smiled back.

"Hey, Lori," he said. "Lookin' good."

It was happening!

"Hey, Topher," I said, trying to act like the girl I thought Topher would want me to be.

"When'd you get here?" he asked me, and I noticed he was perspiring lightly.

"I just got here," I said, trying to come up with a topic of conversation that would keep this boy in front of me, talking forever. But we were rudely interrupted just then by one of Topher's friends racing past us, ready to dive on top of a group of guys sprawled all over a mattress. As the boy landed on top of his friends he yelled at the top of his lungs, "Nigger pile-on!" Then there was raucous laughter.

I was horrified. Mortified. Embarrassed. HURT. I waited to see if the music would suddenly stop and all eyes would turn to me, the only nigger at the party. But nothing happened. In that instant I tried to decide if I should pretend I didn't hear what had just been shouted a mere five feet away from me. Wasn't that what everyone else was doing? Pretending they didn't hear *that* word? Should I act like I had heard but didn't care? Should I laugh? As the only Black person in the basement, perhaps it was my responsibility to explain to the boys why that word is not to be used in a game. But maybe they weren't just playing. Maybe they were trying to tell me something. A million thoughts were rushing through my head as I stood there in front of Topher. He noticed my discomfort and immediately sought to ease my worries.

"They're not talking about you. It's just a game," he said, looking not the least bit embarrassed or worried about my feelings.

"Yeah, I know," I said, shrugging as if standing in a roomful of White kids where the game of choice is "nigger pile-on" was something I did all the time.

"Well, I gotta get back to the game," Topher said.

"Okay, cool," I said. "I'm going to get some more punch. It's really good." I turned away first, but I still heard the scampering of Topher's stocking feet and his voice crying out "Nigger pile-on!" as he rejoined his friends.

I didn't stop at the punch bowl. I headed straight back to the steps and climbed up them. I asked Gloria's mother for the phone so I could call my mother and ask her to pick me up. I told her I was crying because my head hurt. She came right over and picked me up. I never told her what really happened.

In my mind I shelved the nigger pile-on experience alongside the one when I was catching a ride home with Vivian Cole, my bus friend. She lived two blocks away and had seven older brothers and sisters. Occasionally we managed to catch a ride with one of them. This particular day, Vivian and I both sat in the backseat because her sister Lisa's own friend was sitting up front with her. The two of them were seniors in high school. They seemed like real adults to me since I was only ten. Their conversation was of no interest to Vivian and me as we sat in the back and tried to figure out why Matt Schmidt was still coming to school smelling like he peed in his pants.

Lisa had her friend doubling over with guffaws with her joke telling. Their loud voices cut our own laughter short. Vivian and I stopped talking to hear what was so funny.

"I have a better one," Lisa said to her friend. "What does Pontiac stand for?"

"I don't know, what?" the other girl asked.

Lisa could barely get the words out; she was already choked by her own giggles. "Poor. Old. Nigger. Thinks. It's. A. Cadillac." Both of them were laughing now. Hard.

In the backseat my heart started pounding in my ears, my palms grew cold, and I couldn't look at Vivian. She didn't say anything. And the jokes continued in the front seat. I felt ashamed and embarrassed and would have sold my little brother to have gotten out of that car at that instant.

When Lisa pulled her car into my driveway, she didn't yell "Get out, little nigger girl" as I feared she might. Instead she just said, "See ya." Her friend didn't say anything. Vivian said good-bye but wouldn't look me in the eye. I felt bad for her. I didn't want her to think we couldn't be friends anymore. But I was confused. Didn't Vivian's sister know we could hear them? Maybe I wasn't a nigger like she was talking about. Maybe I was different? Special? Maybe she forgot I was Black since I was so good at fitting in with all the Whiteness around me. I decided that was it. I must be so good at blending in, because people all around me seemed to forget that I was Black. So I probably shouldn't hold it against them. I guess people really could be color-blind if they really, really tried. I would just keep trying to keep my Blackness under wraps to keep everything and everyone around me safe and calm.

3: Almost Africa

"Why do I have to go?" I whined at my mother.

"Because your sister is going to France and we have to support AFS." AFS stood for American Field Service, and from what I had gathered, it was an organization that sent American high school students to live in foreign countries. I didn't know much more than that and didn't care to since right now AFS was keeping me from having a respectable social life.

My friends were all going to the movies at the mall followed by pizza at Rocky Rococo, the best deep-dish pizza place in Milwaukee, and I had to go to some dumb potluck with my family at school. The only person I knew who was going to be there was Rachel Smith, the nerdiest girl in my class. Her older sister was going to Switzerland on this AFS exchange program.

"And what does that have to do with me?" I asked as I watched my mother get dressed.

"Look, it's a family potluck, you're part of this family, so stop your moping and go change. You can't go out looking like that."

Now that I was thirteen and a "young woman," my mother didn't want to see me in sweatpants all the time. She cared what other people thought of her offspring, especially when it came to people from our school. Even though she preached a steady sermon on the importance of individuality and the dangers of being part of a "cattle mentality," my mother was acutely aware of the Joneses, and she was damn sure she'd be keeping up.

I dragged my thick teenage body to my room and tried to decide what would be an appropriate outfit for a party I didn't want to attend.

I settled on blue corduroys, a yellow turtleneck, and my fuzzy blue cable-knit sweater with the glass beads. I hoped my mother would approve.

Actually she didn't really have any more time for me and my bad mood. She was getting my brother dressed, yelling at my father to hurry up, and making sure my sister dressed appropriately, choosing nothing too "alternative" that might make the AFS people revoke their decision to allow her to represent America abroad.

The party was being held in the middle-school dining room. With its two large adjoining rooms, a fireplace, and black and white marble floors, it was easily transformed into an elegant party space. When we got there the room was already filled with people. I recognized a few people from school. There was also a contingent of folks with that telltale "not from the city" appearance. Their blue jeans, flannel shirts, and sweater sets in pastel colors screamed Racine, Cudahy, and other far-flung towns in Wisconsin. Sprinkled throughout the room were a bunch of ambiguously tan, brown, and olive-toned kids. These were the AFSers. This was the contingent of international exchange students who had been placed with host families all over Wisconsin and were now experiencing their first big city visit during Milwaukee Weekend. This is what we were celebrating.

I stayed close to my mother, who knew quite a few people at the party. We were introduced to kids from all over the world who all seemed unbelievably nice and excited to meet me. They didn't appear to regard me any differently than the other mostly White people in the mix. I was just another new American friend. I liked that. I also liked the food. Set out on three long tables was a smorgasbord of other people's cultural creations. Usually a potluck in Milwaukee meant eighteen variations on spaghetti, but this was an international feast. Imagine chicken curry, cellophane rice noodles, kuchens both sweet and savory, and a scrumptious assortment of rice-based dishes, one more exotic than the next. After dinner, the tables were cleared from the back part of the room and a bunch of girls from Thailand did a traditional folk dance, followed by Luigi, the Italian boy, playing his violin with such passion I fell in love with him instantly. And just like that, I was hooked. Never before in my thirteen years of life had I felt so instantly at peace and excited and happy with another group of people. This AFS potluck proved to be a portal into the rest of the world for me. Everyone here was from somewhere else, or wanted to go somewhere else, which made me fit right in with the majority. By the time the potluck party was over, I had begged my mom to allow me to accompany the kids on their field trip the next day to the natural history museum and the Miller Beer brewery, Milwaukee's two must-see tourist attractions. Mom said okay. She too got caught up in the rapture. While I was plotting a way to stay involved with this incredible group of international students, she was plotting a way to get involved with the organization on an administrative level. The following Monday, I joined the AFS club at school and Mom became the official home-stay coordinator, in charge of finding families to host the incoming foreign students.

My sister returned from her AFS summer in France eating mustard on her French fries, raisins with her chicken, listening to mournful French music, and rolling her eyes at her family's pathetic lack of worldly sophistication. The fact that she had been living on a farm far from Paris, where dinner was often the roadkill her French father had rolled over that day, seemed to make little difference. She was a woman transformed. She was chic and we were not.

I wanted to change, too. At the beginning of my junior year of high school, my mother asked if I wanted to go on AFS. I couldn't believe she had to ask. Didn't I love all things AFS? Didn't I help assemble two hundred mini ham sandwiches every spring for the AFS Milwaukee Weekend brunch? Didn't I happily give up my room for our weekend AFS visitors every year? Did I not willingly befriend every foreign student temporarily placed in our home (Mom had been promoted to AFS problem solver) when they couldn't get along with their host family?·

"Of course I'm going," I said to my mom.

"Okay, I just wanted to make sure. I never know if you've changed your mind," my mother said.

She had a point. I was a chronic mind-changer, but still, couldn't she tell how AFS was changing my worldview? And changing me? Thanks to all my interactions with teenagers from around the world, I found out how cosmically insignificant America was. I discovered that not all people witnessed every event through the prism of race. And even if they did, the concept of race had a million different definitions, depending on whom I was talking to.

I learned that many teenage boys were completely okay with expressing their feelings through music and art instead of football and fart jokes. I realized that beauty was far more inclusive than blond hair, skinny bodies, and small feet with high arches. Just by befriending these temporary travelers while they spent a weekend in our midst, I had expanded my vision of reality exponentially. So I planned on riding this ride till the end.

"So where do you want to go?" my mom asked.

I had thought long and hard about this. Elisa went to France. So of course everyone would expect me to go to Europe, too, since I generally followed in her footsteps. If not Spain, at the very least South America would be considered safe and predictable, but predictable wasn't something I aspired to be. My modus operandi was "always keep them guessing." When I scoured the list of possible countries to go to, I knew I wanted to see Africa. Not only did I decide as a Black person I should use this opportunity to discover my roots, I rationalized that this would be a great way to trump my sister, who had played it safe by going to Europe. I could definitely beat her on the "wow" factor with an African adventure.

"I'm thinking about Africa," I said aloud to my mom for the first time.

"Africa? Why Africa?" she asked, trying to keep judgment out of her voice.

"Because I want to discover my roots," I answered, knowing my mother would think Africa an unsafe choice.

"Well, where in Africa are you planning on going?" she asked.

"Well, Laverne at school went to Senegal last year, but the program there isn't open anymore. According to the brochure, the only countries in Africa that are open are Morocco and Egypt."

"So . . ." my mom prodded.

"I'm thinking Morocco, because I read that they speak Spanish there, so I can still use my language skills." Truthfully, I knew nothing about Morocco when I saw it there on the list of available African countries. Once I saw in the encyclopedia that they speak Spanish in some northern parts of the country, I made my decision. Even though going to Egypt sounded grand. The pyramids. The palm trees. The history. But to me, Egypt sounded like a place people could go on a tour with the natural history museum. I didn't know anyone who'd been to Morocco. To me, that was a plus. I'd be a pioneer. A first. I'd get the attention for being brave and exotic.

"Okay," my mom said, sounding like I'd just told her I'd decided to wear my hair in one ponytail instead of two.

"Aren't you excited for me?" I asked, expecting more emotion from the woman who constantly worried about the dangers lurking behind every corner thanks to her years working as a pediatric nurse.

"Sure," my mom answered, "but let's see if you get accepted first. And second, you don't always get your first country request."

But I just knew I would. From Milwaukee to Morocco, it sounded too good not to come true. A perfect chapter title in the story of my life.

Apparently not too many American kids were clamoring to be exchange students to Morocco back in 1989, the year I spent three months living with the Khourcha clan in Casablanca. There were only ten of us on the program that summer, compared to the forty-four heading to France. Of that ten, four of us were from Wisconsin, nine of us were girls, and there was one daughter of a famous NBA star.

My first impression of Casablanca was that with its endless palm trees and white stucco houses topped with red Spanish tiled roofs, it looked like Los Angeles.

"Everything is so modern," I said aloud to no one and everyone in the van carrying us from the airport to the American Cultural Center for orientation.

"What? You were expecting camels walking the streets?" snorted

Boubker, our program director. I bit my lip, because in actuality I was. I had this vision that I would find a totally different world in Africa.

"We are not Africans," is what Boubker explained once we were all comfortably seated on the terrace of the American center in the middle of Casablanca. He was giving us the fifteen-minute explanation of Morocco. "We are Arabs," he said proudly. I didn't know what to make of that statement because the last time I checked, Morocco was still attached to the continent of Africa, which would make them Africans. But apparently the Moroccans didn't want the connection made. The dark-skinned "Africans," I would later learn, came from anywhere below Morocco. Usually the "Africans" were the maids and servants in Moroccan homes. So, there went my grand plans to discover my roots. And that wasn't the only thing I wasn't going to discover. I also wasn't going to discover my ability to communicate in Spanish because my host family spoke only Arabic in the house. All of my host sisters and brothers were bilingual in French and Arabic, but my host mother insisted on Arabic. And thus began my adventures as a selective mute.

"Here, try this," Salwa said as she shoved a glass full of what looked and smelled like curdled milk in my face while taking me on a tour through the kitchen. Even knowing the cardinal rule of eating whatever is placed in front of you, I quickly invented a raging allergy to dairy so as not to have to swallow what turned out to be *laben*, a very popular Moroccan drink. Momentarily saved, I continued on the tour as Salwa whisked me around the house, introducing me to my three new brothers and eight sisters while simultaneously pointing out the beauty and wealth of their home. "That's Ibitisam and Hassan over there," she'd say, then drag me to the next room, where she'd pull out a piece of luxurious embroidered silk. "All by hand," Salwa said with pride. "Come touch it. Is it not beautiful?" I was so overwhelmed I could only nod and pat at the beautiful material.

The Mansouri home sat on the opposite side of the city from where the rest of the American AFS students had been placed. While they all lived within walking distance of one another in the "Western" part of the city—where the most exotic thing around might have been the well-manicured jasmine bushes—I was living almost an hour away by bus in what seemed like a very poor part of town. Our front yard was a gas station, and when I peered out the window from a second-floor window, I could see a shantytown.

Salwa finished the tour at what would be my bedroom, which was actually the family room, furnished only with a couch and a traditional round Moroccan coffee table.

"You will sleep here," Salwa said in her perfect English, gesturing to the brown, lumpy sofa that stretched around the entire perimeter of the room. "But you will keep all of your belongings hidden in Nahid and Hind's room." Nahid and Hind were my youngest sisters. They thought my butchered rendition of "hello" in Arabic was hilarious and immediately tried to help me speak properly when they met me. I think they liked me. Unlike my older sisters, the ones my age, who barely glanced in my direction when we were introduced.

Tour over, Salwa handed me a small book. "This is a Moroccan Arabic dictionary. Memorize it so you can communicate better here," she said.

I started to laugh. "You want me to memorize a dictionary?" I said. "Are you kidding?"

She wasn't. Salwa was completely serious.

"You Americans think everyone should learn your language. Why is that? You are the richest country and your people speak only one language."

She had a point.

"How many languages do you speak?" she asked me.

"One," I said, feeling shameful as I said it.

"I speak Arabic, French, English, and German," Salwa said, ticking them off on her fingers. "My little sisters speak two languages and are learning English. You will memorize this book," she said again. I gathered that this wasn't a suggestion. It was an order.

I took the book from her hand and promised to do my best. Apparently satisfied, she left me to go pray. I was instructed to unpack.

I went into my room, threw myself on my couch-bed, and cried like a baby. What had I done? What had I gotten myself into? Why didn't I choose "predictable" and go to Spain?

I didn't memorize the dictionary, although Salwa continued to check on my progress every day. "What page are you on?" she liked to ask me. I never made it past page 10. Luckily, she didn't hold it against me. Instead, Salwa cared for me like a mother hen, making sure I was always safe and well taken care of. She was the only sister out of the eight who spoke fluent English, so she was my self-appointed guardian. But she couldn't stick by my side every day. She had her own trip to prepare for. In the fall, Salwa was going to be an exchange student to the United States.

Many days I was left alone while Salwa went off to stand in line for visas or shop for winter clothing she would need in Alaska. (Yes, they sent the poor girl to Alaska.) And of course there were the five times a day she disappeared to pray to Allah. So after two weeks of crippling culture shock, spending entire days alone in my room writing letters to my friends back home, I decided to venture out into the wilds of Casablanca.

I had to fight with Naima, my oldest sister, first. She didn't think it was safe to have the dumb American girl alone on the streets. She called me into her room and asked me to help her spread body lotion on her back. In her halting but functional English she explained why I would not be allowed to leave the house, even though I had already made plans to meet my American friend Lucy in town.

"It is too dangerous and we are responsible for you," she said.

"But I'm seventeen. I can take care of myself," I said, even though I was secretly terrified to venture out and ride the bus to the American Cultural Center. What if I got lost? Or what if somebody plunged a knife into my back? But greater than that fear was the sense of imprisonment I felt in that house, where nothing felt familiar.

"You will not go alone. If you want, when I return home from work, I will take you out for an excursion."

I felt the tears prickling behind my eyelids. I needed to leave this place, had worked up the courage to venture out, and now this woman, who up until now had barely spoken to me, was telling me I couldn't go. I felt defeated. I didn't have the words to plead my case. And technically I was a guest in this home and I had to do what I was told.

Then Salwa came whooshing in to save the day.

"What's going on in here?" she asked, taking in her half-naked sister, the lotion on my hands, and the tears beginning to fall down my cheeks.

Before I had a chance to explain, Naima launched into what sounded like an angry tirade. But Arabic always sounded kind of angry to my untrained ear.

Salwa answered back in turn, and it sounded like she was arguing in my favor, but I couldn't tell, because tragically, I was still only on page 10 of that dictionary.

When it was over, Naima had her back well lotioned and I was allowed to go. But Salwa was to accompany me to the bus stop to make sure I got on the right one. Which turned out to be a good thing because riding the bus in Morocco is an adventure. Dressed in a djellaba that covered my American clothes, I blended into the crowd, especially with my brown skin. I was treated like a native, which meant when the bus pulled up to the stop, I was pushed and shoved and jostled like everyone else determined to get on the bus.

Completely blowing my cover, Salwa yelled to me in English, "Remember to call when you get there. And you must be home by four o'clock." Feeling like a child off to school for the first time, I tried not to make eye contact with any of the hundred Moroccans on the bus now staring at me.

Salwa told me my stop was the fifth one after crossing the railroad tracks. I counted stops faithfully under my breath. Bodies were crushed all around me, and the stench of human sweat and funk was overwhelming. I knew I didn't want to miss my stop. Apparently that wasn't even a possibility because the driver yelled out "*Americania, Americania!*" when we arrived at my stop. Again, all eyes were on me as I pushed my way to the front of the bus and out the door, but not before squeaking out a heartfelt "*shukran*" to the driver.

Deposited in the heart of Casablanca, I felt free and refreshed. The city, though hardly similar to Milwaukee, offered familiar comforts. I recognized clothing boutiques and bookstores, restaurants and cafés. I stopped at a bakery around the corner from the cultural center and bought a raisin Danish and a cold Coke in one of those old-fashioned glass bottles. The sugar and white flour provided a welcome sensation in my partially starved and dehydrated body. Eating and drinking had become a problem for me. In the Mansouri household, the big meal of the day came at midday and usually involved lamb. Unfortunately, at that time in my life, I hated lamb.

We ate as a family around a low round table and we ate with our hands. Actually only one hand, the right one, was allowed on the table. I grew quite adept at pretending to pull meat off the communal plate, but usually I just ate bread. I didn't like the heavy harissa soup that started every meal, either, and I feared drinking from the one communal cup of tap water placed on the table. And of course Mommy, who sat at the head of the table, wasn't too pleased with my attitude and manners. I wasn't endearing myself to anyone.

As I rounded the corner, licking the last bit of Danish from my fingers, Lucy came flying at me, her fiery red hair and freckled face the most beautiful sight in the world. I almost cried with happiness. We hugged each other, both laughing at our families' similar attempts at "disguising" us, making us wear djellabas. Lucy's family situation was even weirder than mine. Her original family decided at the last minute they didn't want an exchange student, so Boubker had to scramble and found a young couple with a newborn baby to host Lucy. Lucy's "mother" was only three years older than Lucy, but her husband was in his midforties. They too lived away from the ritzy neighborhood where the rest of the group found themselves staying.

Lucy held me at arm's length.

"What happened to you?" she asked me, frowning. "You look terrible."

"I do?" I said.

"Yeah, you look skinny and your skin looks kind of gray. And you just look sad," she said.

"Is it that obvious?" I said, patting my hair self-consciously.

"Yeah, what's the matter? What's going on?" Lucy looked really concerned, and her concern made me want to cry. As I looked at my new friend I noticed that the opposite was true of her. She looked truly radiant, even more full of life than when we had first met back in New York at orientation.

I opened my mouth to give an explanation for my pitiful appearance and an avalanche of emotion came pouring out. "I'm so miserable. I'm starving all the time because we only eat lamb and I hate lamb and there's only one glass of water on the table for everyone to drink out of and I'm too afraid to ask for bottled water and all my sisters hate me except for Salwa and the other morning I heard one of the maids being beaten and I tripped over a sheep's hoof in the street on my way here."

And then I really started to cry.

Lucy ushered me over to a bench in front of the cultural center and let me cry. When I was done, I tried to laugh it off. "You, on the other hand, look marvelous," I said. "What's your secret? Are you actually happy here?" I said.

"Yeah," Lucy said. "I'm loving it. I mean yes, I think I picked up some bug from the water, but I'm just taking lots of Imodium for that, and yes, my host mother is more like a sister with this husband who's like forty who is such a bore, but the baby is really cute and I'm helping out with him. I'm just throwing myself into everything."

"Are you eating all the food?" I asked.

"Yes."

"And you're drinking the regular tap water?"

"Yeah."

"And you're still alive," I said in mock disbelief. We had been repeatedly warned by our AFS representatives in the States not to drink the water. I had seen bottled water in the Khourcha kitchen but hadn't felt comfortable asking for it since nobody else was drinking it.

"Okay, I think I know what you need to do. You have to just stop being afraid of everything and just go for it. We're only here for a couple months. You'll never have this opportunity again."

It all sounded so easy. I thought about Lucy's advice as I rode the bus back home. I had a seat this time and tried to imagine feeling as happy as Lucy looked. I wanted that. I had imagined an experience like that when I had been filling out the application forms to come to Morocco. And now here I was being a big party pooper. By the time the bus arrived at my stop, there were just a handful of people left. I walked to the front of the bus and said "*shukran*" again and smiled instead of rushing off. He smiled back and said, "*Zwīna bezzef*"—"Very beautiful." And I continued to smile all the way home.

Lucy was right. Eating lamb and drinking the water made all the difference in the world. I gained entrée into the heart of Moroccan culture and my family by happily eating lamb tagine every day, learning how to while away hours sipping glass after glass of sweet mint tea, and sitting around the table after dinner while my family tried to teach me increasingly difficult words in Arabic. I was the after-dinner entertainment. But I now felt the warm embrace of the entire family. Except for my one brother Mohammed, who, at twenty-five, was suspicious of my female intentions. When we were alone in a room he would tell me I had to leave because "between a man and a woman there is Satan."

Although she prayed five times a day and was a devout Muslim herself, Salwa didn't buy into her brother's ideas of Satan lurking between the sexes. I knew this to be true because one day two of her friends made a surprise visit. And they were boys! Said and Waffa came upstairs and were ushered into the salon, which ten minutes before had been my bedroom. Waffa was kind of round and thick; his skin was the color of cinnamon. My first impression of Said was that he looked like an Arabic Kirk Cameron. He had olive-toned skin, big round eyes, and a head full of shiny black curls. I fell for him instantly. And the feeling, it seemed, was mutual.

Both boys had come over to meet "the American," and I loved being the center of attention as they plied me with questions about Levi's, Michael Jackson, and New York City. I didn't know much about any of those topics, but that didn't stop me from making up the answers. Like Salwa, they spoke English very well, with only a few mistakes here and there. Was it just me or was Said fixing those magnificent eyes on me for longer and longer periods of time? I giggled and flirted shamelessly, talking without coming up for air. Salwa seemed pleased to show me off like a trophy, plus I was giving her friends a chance to practice their English. I didn't want the moment to end. But after four glasses of tea each and an entire bowl of grapes, there wasn't much more to say. The boys had to leave, but we promised we'd get together again. Salwa and I walked them to the stairs and watched them start down. Suddenly, Said turned around and came flying back up the stairs.

"Would you like to meet me sometime?" he asked me, grabbing my hand.

I looked at Salwa to see if she was okay with this. Her face looked blank.

I turned back to Said and answered truthfully: "I'd love to." He then said something rapidly in Arabic to Salwa, and she mumbled something in return to Said. She didn't sound too pleased, and I wondered if I had misspoken. Maybe Said was Salwa's boyfriend, or worse, maybe she had a crush on him too!

Said smiled at me then, and I couldn't have cared less if he was engaged to marry Salwa. In this moment he was mine. Never in my seventeen years had a boy that I had actually had a crush on returned my affections. I never dared to voice my love to the White boys who populated my school, and the two Black boys in my grade, recent recruits from the public school system, weren't my type. Halfway around the world and I had found my Prince Charming, complete with sexy accent. Maybe Mohammed was right. Stand back Satan!

For our "date," Salwa told me I was to meet Said in front of the little grocery store about a block from our house. They had arranged everything. Salwa wasn't mad at me for going out with Said, but she didn't want Said to think I was an easy American girl. I assured Salwa that there wasn't anything easy about me. I told her I had never even kissed a boy, making it sound more like it had been my choice as opposed to an absolute lack of opportunity. She seemed very happy to hear that and started to get excited for me go out with Said.

I decided to wear my white linen culottes with my yellow and purple short-sleeved blouse. I looked conservative yet feminine, I thought. I only had to wait for about two minutes before Said arrived. I had no idea what a date meant to a Moroccan teenager. I envisioned us going into the center of the city and sipping orange sodas at an outdoor café, like the one Lucy and I had discovered. Or maybe we'd stroll around the park. For a moment I worried that Said might think he was going to get some action with the American, but I quickly banished that thought, assuming Salwa would never associate with that type of person. She was too religious. Still, since I'd been venturing out alone, it had become increasingly clear that Moroccan men believed American women came in one variety, rich and easy. Regardless of race, color, or good looks. If I wasn't hiding under my djellaba, I couldn't walk down the street without hearing dozens of catcalls and cries of "*Zwīna, zwīna bezzef.* Marry me, American princess!" Even though I was Black, my style of dress and my relaxed hair gave me away as an American. And as an American, I instantly qualified as a hot commodity. It was a new sensation to be universally heralded as desirable, and I had to admit I found the attention flattering. I knew it was my perceived American money and thoughts of easy sex that were the most alluring part of the package, as evidenced by the fact that even the homely American AFS girl with a full beard had a handful of serious admirers and one devoted boyfriend. Still, I felt the thrill of not being sidelined from the beauty contest just because I was Black. I was an equal. But just in case God was taking notes, I always acted annoyed by it all.

"*Salaam alaikum,*" Said said in greeting.

We kissed on both cheeks, as was the custom, but this time I felt a shiver of excitement as he drew near. I wondered if he did as well. As if it was the most usual thing in the world, Said reached for my hand and we started walking. I didn't dare ask where we were going as I had learned that asking questions in Morocco never yielded a satisfying answer. All things became clear in good time. So even though I was desperate to know where we were heading, I acted like I had not a care in the world and was happy to stroll hand in hand with Said Hamiriti. After some awkward small talk, Said said he was taking me to meet his mother. Already? I thought to myself. This felt like a big step for our first official rendezvous.

When we reached his home, it was painfully clear that Said's family enjoyed nowhere near the same level of wealth as the Mansouri clan. Said, his parents, and two brothers shared a small apartment. When his mother came out of the kitchen to meet me, she wore a typical shapeless Moroccan housedress and her head was wrapped in a scarf. She did not seem pleased to meet me. She placed a pot of mint tea on the table in front of the couch we were all seated on without looking me in the eye. I spewed out my three lines of Arabic: "Hello. How are you? And God is great, isn't he?" Once that was over the three of us sat there in awkward silence. Said's mother spoke no English, I was still stuck on page 10 of that dictionary, and Said seemed at a loss as to how to bridge the vast communication gap between us. So he just sat there. And that's when I knew it was over between us. I could never find happiness with a boy content to sit in silence. If I had been in America I would have cracked a joke. Complimented the cloying sweetness of the tea. Told the story of my first attempt at eating with chopsticks. But without the gift of language, I felt stupid and useless. And truth be told, in Said's little apartment, a wee bit bored.

What seemed like several hours later but was really only one, Said announced that the visit was over. After saying good-bye in Arabic we made our retreat. I let out an audible sigh of relief once we were outside. Said told me his mother liked me. "How could you tell?" I demanded. Said looked sheepish. I don't think he had a clue, but he wanted her to like me. "You are so beautiful," he said instead, and I immediately forgave his wishful thinking. I tried to blush and smile demurely. "I think I want to marry you," he said. My heart skipped a beat. Was this really happening to me? A handsome stranger from an exotic land was about to make me his wife? This was just as good as the story lines in the romance novels I'd been devouring since discovering my aunt's secret stash of Harlequins in her attic. I knew my quiet patience waiting for a happy ending would be rewarded with something on a grand scale, like becoming a Moroccan princess. Only Said wasn't a prince. And if I married him, I'd probably be in the kitchen with a scarf on my head making tea for guests, still trying to memorize my dictionary. No thanks!

I think Said saw the concern on my face. Rather than take back his marriage proposal, he said, "I love you." Now I was getting rather nervous. We'd only spent an hour staring at the wall together in the presence of his mother and he'd fallen in love? In my heart of hearts I'd always suspected I was irresistible to men, it was just that those boring Milwaukee boys were too blinded by blond to see it, but Said was freaking me out.

"Come, I will take you home now," he said, reaching for my hand again.

This time my hand felt imprisoned in his. The walk back was silent. When we reached the front door of my house Said smiled at me and much to my horror repeated his desire to marry me.

"But I'll have to ask my mother first if she approves," he said, his forehead wrinkling in worry.

I didn't know if he was really serious, but just in case I thought I ought to make myself understood.

"Said, I'm too young to get married. I'm not even done with high school," I said.

"I will wait for you," he said. Like he really meant it. "I have to finish my studies, too."

This conversation was so surreal I just nodded my head as if that made sense. Said leaned in and kissed me on both cheeks again and turned around and walked back the way we came.

It had been my first date and had ended with my first marriage proposal. Not bad. Not bad at all.

I avoided Said for the rest of my visit in Morocco. Which wasn't hard since with three weeks left in my stay, the Mansouri family decided they wanted me to see as much of their country as humanly possible. Every weekend we spent at their beach house outside of Casablanca.

Sometimes I'd meet up with some of the other American AFSers whose families also owned beachfront property.

Salwa also took me to visit relatives in small coastal towns like El Jadida and in the capital of Rabat. Everywhere we went, I could expect at least ten men to comment on my beauty. I received several more marriage proposals from complete strangers, and one time a man followed Salwa, Lucy, and me home, begging us to stop and speak to him so he could practice his English. When we refused to stop and review verbs and vocabulary with him, he changed tactics. He started taunting us, walking right behind us, shouting. "His eyes were like mine!" he roared. "But the kid is not my son!" One more line and I realized that our stalker was shouting the lyrics of Michael Jackson's "Billie Jean." I clapped my hand over my mouth to keep from laughing out loud, lest he take offense and attack us on the deserted road.

By the time I left Morocco, I was ten pounds lighter thanks to the parasites now living happily in my gut. I could speak enough Arabic to make it through customs without the guards knowing I wasn't a native of their country, and I had mastered eating couscous with one hand. More important, I had experienced a world outside of my reality, where the color of my skin didn't define me. My Americanness did. I liked that much better. Now I knew for sure that I wanted to continue traveling the world. I wanted to see if only in America would I be forced to define myself by a collective history. I wondered what I would be or could be in Spain.

4: Quique

Returning to Milwaukee after two and a half months in Casablanca felt like eating lukewarm oatmeal. Gray, cold, and tasteless. I missed the adventure, the newness, and the color of everything in Morocco. I missed being special everywhere I went. I missed being told I was beautiful every time I walked out of my house. In fact, every time I entered a room or ventured outside, I boldly stared at the men around me, wondering why they weren't falling down at my feet professing their love as so many of my Moroccan admirers had. Yes, life was back to normal.

I had my senior year of high school to consume my time. My parents had moved to a new house deep in the woodsy suburbs of Milwaukee, where our closest neighbors were a friendly family of deer and an occasional fox. And my little brother had developed a personality that seemed to revolve around annoying me. Most pressing on my agenda, however, was the stack of college applications waiting to be filled out. Only three weeks back from Morocco and my life already felt like a pressure cooker waiting to explode.

The only thing I had to look forward to was the Spanish exchange program debuting at our high school. Spearheaded by the new Spanish teacher, Señora Spector, the program was announced soon after the school year began. Eleven kids from Madrid were coming to stay with families from our school for a month, and then eleven of us would head to Spain in the spring, live with families, and attend school. Unlike in Mr. Betancourt's spring break pleasure trips, Sra. Spector explained, the kids selected for this program would have to be good students who took Spanish seriously. You couldn't just go because your parents put up the cash. Profe, as we called her, was serious about language learning. She was an American, but I'd never heard her speak a single word of English, and for that I loved her. And for my unceasing passion and enthusiasm for the Spanish language, she loved me, too.

Before Profe finished detailing the particulars of the program I knew I wanted to go. I was the president of the Spanish club, so how would it look if I didn't participate? Besides, I needed to spruce up my Spanish, which had been horribly contaminated with bits of French and Arabic. I couldn't stop answering Profe's questions with a *oui* and thanking her with a *shukran* instead of *gracias*. Not to mention, another trip abroad would look great on my college applications. When I told my parents about the program, they both agreed it sounded like a good idea, too, in theory. They promised nothing, but agreed to keep an open mind about the idea.

I was okay with my parents' wait-and-see attitude. I too wanted to see what these people from Spain would be like. I didn't ask my parents if we could host one of them, even though that would have improved my chances of being selected to go to Spain in the spring. Secretly, I was worried that the students might not want to stay with a Black family, especially a Black family who didn't have an enormous house, hired help, and fancy cars like some of the students at my school. I reasoned that it wasn't fair to put them in a house like ours when they could have a chance to live like royalty with some other family. I told myself I was thinking of their needs, but really I was protecting myself from rejection.

Once they arrived, *los españoles* seemed to be everywhere. They were easy to spot in the hallways at school. The boys all wore gray wool slacks, button-down shirts, and navy blue sweaters. The girls wore the same, sporting wool skirts instead of pants. It seemed that they had cast a spell on the whole school, enchanting everyone with their playful antics and lispy accents. Everyone wanted to play basketball with Quique, gossip with Carolina, teach Juan Luis to play football *americano*. The American boys all fell in love with the gorgeous María, and every girl, even the plainest among us, felt beautiful under the flirtatious attention of the Spanish boys.

As the president of the Spanish club, I tried to be everywhere *los españoles* were. It was almost like an obsession. I wanted their foreignness to surround me. I wanted to be enveloped in their otherworldliness and forget about calculus homework, my GPA, and essay questions that required the meaning of life to be explained in a tidy five hundred words. Having the Spanish students around gave me an excuse to focus on the whole world instead of just my world. I felt enlightened when I was with them. My entire sense of what mattered had shifted from my insignificant life issues to keeping up with these eleven kids from across the ocean. Being with them gave me a taste of their world, and I was so very hungry for new flavors.

"What do you mean you're not coming?" my best friend Krista shrieked over the telephone.

"Um, yeah, can you give my ticket to someone else or sell it maybe?" I asked, feeling only slightly guilty about dissing my two best friends and our plans to see R.E.M. in concert that night. I had spent the entire day in Chicago with *them*, and since nobody wanted the funfest to end, an impromptu party had been arranged.

"I mean, yeah, we can probably scalp it," Krista said with obvious annoyance in her voice.

"Krisstaaa," I pleaded, deciding I had to be totally honest in order for her to support my decision. "You know Quique is going to be at the party and we had such a good time in Chicago today and they're going to be gone in like a week. I have to do this."

Krista and Erin were on a mission to lose their virginity before senior year ended. Both of them were well on their way to success. They looked at me with my absolutely chaste life and were determined to change things posthaste. I knew that the idea of me getting some action would make Krista sympathetic to my sudden change in plans.

"Okay," Krista said, relenting. "But you better jump his bones tonight," she said, "or else I'll never forgive you for missing this concert."

"Jump his bones"? I wouldn't even know where to start, I thought as I got dressed for the party. I got embarrassed just thinking about it. I didn't even know if Quique liked me like that. I kind of got the feeling that something was going on because he seemed to be flirting with me. Like when a bunch of us sneaked off campus to go have lunch at my friend Ann's house the other day, the conversation turned to kissing. We were trying to define French kissing for Quique, María, and Carolina, who had come with us. Quique then looked directly at me when he said, "I don't know why they call it French kissing. It should be called Spanish kissing because we are much better at it than the French." I had to turn away from his gaze when he said that. And then all day in Chicago we had walked and talked together as we visited Chicago's major tourist attractions like the Field Museum and the Shedd Aquarium. We sat together on the bus ride home and he told me about his love of basketball and his secret hobby of writing poetry. But still, how would I know if this constituted an interest in me as a friend or a potential girlfriend? Maybe he just liked practicing his English. Maybe he wouldn't even consider kissing a black person. He was, after all, the only blond-haired, green-eyed Spaniard in the bunch. Many times in the past four years of my life as a teenager, I thought I felt something special between myself and a boy, only to have nothing come of it.

All of these thoughts raced through my brain as I got ready. Satisfied with my outfit of khaki pants, a T-shirt, and one of my signature men's vests, I told my mother I was ready to go. Having failed my driver's test not once, but twice, I was still dependent on Mom for taxi shuttle service.

The party was in full swing when I got there. The McCormick family home was perfect for teenage gatherings. Full basement with carpet, couches, and a state-of-the-art stereo system. Kids were in the basement and running around outside. No parents were around, but James McCormick's ancient grandmother was holed up in her room upstairs, so technically the party had adult supervision. I went to the basement and found most of the Spaniards and a lot of American groupies like me. Some kids were playing pool; others were examining the extensive collection of records that lined one entire wall from top to bottom. I spoke to Carolina and Aranxa. Watched Andy try to make his move on María (and from the looks of things, it was working). I got some punch, making sure it wasn't spiked by dipping my tongue in and testing for the bitter taste of alcohol. Unlike at most parties that defined my high school years, people weren't drinking themselves silly and everybody wasn't White. It was like the Spaniards had brought out the colorful and interesting. I was in heaven. But then I noticed Quique wasn't there.

I patrolled the entire basement, asking around without trying to be too obvious if anyone had seen him. Nobody had. I wondered if maybe he wasn't coming. His host family did live really far away, on a farm out in Grafton, but they'd been good about bringing him to all the extracurricular activities we'd planned. Maybe tonight's party didn't warrant the forty-minute drive. My heart sank. I thought about Michael Stipe and cursed myself for putting a boy in front of a great night out with my girls.

"Lori."

I turned to find Carolina, the tiny Spanish imp who made it her business to know everyone else's business, standing behind me.

"Hola," I said, trying to muster up some of my previous happiness.

"Er, you need to go upstairs. Someone is waiting for you."

She wouldn't say who, but of course we both knew I knew.

I climbed up the basement steps and wandered around the house looking for Quique and admiring the exquisite furniture and spacious rooms. I felt a twinge of guilt for "trespassing," but then I saw Quique seated at the piano and forgot about everything else. His back was to me and he looked like he was about to cry, hunched over the keyboard. I sat down next to him.

"What's the matter?" I asked. *"¿Estás bien?"*

"I have a problem," he said. "And I don't know how to say it."

"Well," I coached him, thinking he didn't have the words in English to express himself, "just do the best you can, or try in Spanish." I'd never seen him look so sad. I couldn't imagine what had happened since our great trip to Chicago that could have changed his demeanor so.

With an exasperated sigh, he said with quiet desperation, "I love you."

My world stopped. My ears started to ring. My skin went cold and my face went hot. I couldn't swallow.

"What?" I said, reeling in shock and amazement.

He turned to me then and said it three times fast. "I love you. I love you. I love you." He took my hand and, caressing it like it was a rare jewel, said, "You are the most beautiful person I've ever met and you make me feel something I cannot know the words for. You're smart and that smile and that body and everything is so good. I just love you so much."

I didn't know what to say. Quique seemed so tortured with this love for me, I wanted to wrap my arms around him and soothe his tortured heart . . . but before I could decide what to do, he leaned over and kissed me on the mouth. And then he did it again. And we sat there kissing on the piano bench in the dark and I couldn't help but think how glad I was that I wasn't watching an R.E.M. concert.

When I floated home, I took a shower and wrapped myself up in my cozy pink terry-cloth robe. I found my mother in the basement doing laundry.

"How was the party?" she asked me as she sorted the darks from the lights.

"It was wonderful," I said, wondering if my voice betrayed my emotions. Apparently it did, because my mom turned to get a better look at me.

"What happened?" she asked me, looking at me quizzically with a raised eyebrow. No longer interested in dirty clothes.

Without leaving out a single detail, I told her exactly what had happened.

"He loves me, Mom," I squealed. "What do you think I should do?"

"Did you tell him that you loved him back?" my mother asked me.

"No," I said.

"Why not?" she asked.

"Because I don't even know if I know what love is," I commented.

"Well, the way I see it, the boy is only going to be here another week and you could make him really happy."

"You want me to lie?" I said, aghast at my mother's suggestion.

"Well, do you love him?" she asked.

"I mean yeah, I guess so." And then I thought about how I felt when Quique was around and how sweet and funny he was and how much he loved me and I decided I did love him. I didn't have to lie.

"I have to tell him," I said to my mother and myself with a hugely satisfied grin on my face.

I didn't want to tell Quique on the phone how I felt because when two people don't speak the same mother tongue, telephone conversations can feel awkward. I vowed to wait only till Monday morning.

In the meantime, I replayed Saturday night over and over and over again in my mind. The falling star we witnessed together while sitting in the middle of the street marveling at how we met. Our plans to enjoy every minute of our time together. The sweet kisses—which Krista later informed me didn't count because no tongues were involved. Still, my wannabe slutty friends were proud of me and forgave me for ditching them.

Before I got a chance to spill my guts to Quique at school, little Carolina passed me a note during our history class, which she was visiting. It was so sixth grade, but I felt a ridiculous thrill anyway when I opened the crumpled piece of notebook paper. On it she had written: "What happened the Saturday with Enrique? Do you like Enrique?"

I wrote back: *"¿Por qué tú preguntas?"* Why do you ask?

And she wrote: "Because on the Sunday my Spanish friends told me that you and Enrique are love and love. I think so because Enrique told me that he like you. And now he needs to know do you like Enrique?"

And I wrote back: *"Claro que sí."*

I felt bad that Quique didn't know how much I liked him . . . I mean, loved him. My next period was free. I found Quique in the hall and dragged him to the theater, where I knew we could be alone for a few minutes before assembly. We went backstage behind the curtains and I said, "I couldn't wait any longer. I want you to know that I love you, too. I really do."

"And I love you," he said.

And then we kissed. A lot. With tongue. And I felt a delicious thrill until I heard people filing into the auditorium for assembly. I pushed Quique away from me and told him to go out the door on stage left. I waited an extra minute and snuck out back and reentered the auditorium through the front door, a woman in love. A woman loved.

The rest of the week passed by frustratingly quickly. A whirl of stolen kisses in the back of the theater and after school in empty classrooms. And it seemed everyone in the school gave us their approval. Winking at me, slapping Quique on the back. And I was happy. Quique couldn't tell me enough times in one day how beautiful I was, and if I dared criticize myself for not doing well on a test or not having any desire to finish with my college applications he encouraged me with kind words of support. And even if he just talked about how much he liked American music, it sounded so sexy with his lispy Spanish accent. (Did I mention I'm a sucker for a guy with an accent?)

On the night before the Spaniards left, a big going-away party was planned. Everyone knew I was going to be miserable. People I had never spoken to before were coming up to me in the hallways at school, offering a shoulder to cry on. Our picture made it into the school paper and my senior yearbook. Quique and I had become the school's romantic mascot. To me, I was living a romance more beautifully tragic than *Romeo and Juliet,* which we had just finished reading in English class. Something this powerful happened only once in a great while and only to a chosen few, I reasoned. It was why I had to wait so long, why I'd been alone and unkissed throughout my entire high school career. Cupid was preparing my heart so I would be ready for my three weeks with Quique.

For the party I wore a teal blue miniskirt with a matching crop top. I wore a black tank top underneath because I didn't want to look slutty, but truth be told, I chose the miniskirt for easy access without having to get undressed. It made sense to me in kind of a puritan tease kind of way. Quique and I had already decided that our last night would be one to remember. All of those stolen kisses and that furtive rubbing against each other in school had been less than satisfying. I had gone from completely virginal to raging horndog in a matter of days. Jonathan, whose house the party was at, had taken pity on us and had arranged for us to be alone in one of the upstairs bedrooms. As soon as possible we both snuck up there.

I sat down on one of the twin beds in what I assumed was Jonathan's older sister's room. I felt a twinge of guilt for what I was about to do in the room of a girl who had been my sister's best friend in the fourth grade. But then I brushed the feeling aside, reasoning that true love trumped fourth-grade friendship any day.

"Hello," Quique said, as if we were meeting for the first time.

"Hola," I said back. Playing along.

Quique walked around the room nervously touching things, the doll on the dresser, the extra pillows on the bed. He peeked behind the doors and found a bathroom. When he came out of the bathroom I had lain down on the bed.

"May I come over?" he said.

I could tell he was nervous. Maybe more than I was, and that made me calm down.

I patted the bed beside me and we lay there together listening to the voices of our friends outside, enjoying the party. I wondered if Andy and María were in another room in this enormous house doing the same thing.

As I lay next to Quique, fat tears started to escape from my eyes. I had promised myself I wouldn't ruin our last night by crying. Quique turned to me, tears in his eyes as well. I loved him so much more then. He kissed my tears and then kissed my mouth and then spread kisses all over my body. Soon clothes started coming off. My shirt. The tank top. His shirt.

Almost an hour later, Quique finally asked. "Do you want to make love?"

Without pausing, I said, "No."

"¿Por qué no?" he said, reverting to Spanish, his face flushed with eagerness.

"Because I'm not ready yet," I said. "And I don't feel like we have to go there to show how much we love each other."

I wanted to give Quique my body to remember me by, but I wasn't even remotely interested in sex. I was afraid it would hurt. And I didn't want to think about the responsibility and the annoyance of, ugh, condoms. I just liked the thrill of fooling around. And so we fooled around some more until Quique had to excuse himself and go to the bathroom, looking like he was in extreme agony.

When he came back out he seemed at ease.

We both knew the inevitable was coming. We could already hear people downstairs starting to say good-bye. We could feel the sadness pulsating in waves all around us. We didn't try to stop our tears this time.

"You won't forget me, will you?" I said to Quique, who had wrapped me in his arms on that skinny twin bed.

"How is it possible to forget your heart? Your soul?" he said to me.

I started bawling then. It just didn't seem fair that I had patiently waited my whole life for this kind of perfect person, this boy who loved to laugh and joke and who wasn't embarrassed to cry and who spoke from his heart and couldn't tell me enough how much he loved being with me. I had found him and he picked *me* and not any of the blond-haired, blue-eyed girls who ran my school. And now, he had to leave. Where was the justice?

"I'm not going to Spain," Quique said. "I am going to live forever in Milwaukee, Wisconsin."

"What about your family?" I asked

"I don't care about them," he said. And I wanted to believe him. But of course he'd be on that plane tomorrow and then . . . And then what?

"I have to come to Spain in the spring," I said, hoping that wanting it bad enough would make it come true.

We kissed and cried until there was a knock at the door. Jonathan didn't come in, he just called through the door, saying that Quique's host family was looking for him because they were ready to leave.

"I'm not coming to say good-bye at the airport," I sobbed dramatically to Quique as he put his shirt back on and fished for his shoes under the bed. "I can't stand saying good-bye at airports. I want this to be our good-bye."

"Okay. Then I have to give you this now," he said, coming back to sit next to me on the bed, his own tears wetting his cheeks. He took off his leather bracelet that I'd admired on the first day we met. "Keep this on until you see me again," he said, tying it on my wrist. "I love you, Lori

Tharps. Stay sweet." And with that, he practically flew out of the room, and I thought I would never see my one true love ever again.

The next morning, my mom kept watch over me like a concerned mother duck. She never let me out of her sight. "Are you sure you don't want to go to the airport?" she kept asking me. "I don't mind driving you." Even my mother understood that I wasn't just playing the part of wounded lover. She hated driving, and going to the airport meant crossing the dreaded Sixth Street Bridge and navigating the highway, which was something she avoided like the plague. I couldn't stop the tears from welling up again at the thought that even my mother felt the love. This was real.

"No," I sighed, but I began to wonder if I was being too stubborn, refusing to say good-bye at the airport. But I knew I'd be a slobbering mess and I didn't want the other kids to see me like that and I didn't want Quique to remember me like that. Still, as I watched the minutes go by on the clock, I tried to imagine their every movement up until departure time.

By 9:30 a.m., I figured they all must be assembled at Milwaukee's General Mitchell Airport, getting their luggage checked in. I started to rethink my mom's offer. If we left right now, we might actually make it. And I'd dash around the airport until I found Quique and we'd have one of those TV-movie moments of laughter and tears and me spinning around in his arms. The doorbell interrupted my fantasy.

"Lori, it's for you," I heard my mom call from the front hallway.

Still in my pink bathrobe, I shuffled to the door and there was Quique, a huge grin on his face.

"What are you doing here?" I asked, wondering how my dreams could come true. "Did you miss your plane?" I asked, hoping he'd say yes.

"No," he said. "I just had to see you one last time and I begged Mrs. Haus to bring me here." I looked behind Quique and sure enough there was Mrs. Haus in her Jeep Cherokee waiting in our driveway. I smiled and waved. She waved back.

"Listen to this and think about me," Quique said, placing a cassette tape in my hands. He kissed me then and ran back to the car.

And that was that.

I listened to the tape, an eclectic mix of Quique's favorite songs, including a karaoke version of "The Lady in Red" sung by Quique himself. I played the song over and over until my family demanded I stop. His first letter to me came a week later with a tracing of his hand on the envelope and a note that said, "This is my handprint, touch me now!" The letters, filled with longing and sadness and pledges of eternal love, came almost every other week. And I returned each one with equal fervor. In between writing letters, I wrote essays to get into college even though I really just wanted to run away to Spain and be a bohemian and love Quique. I applied and was accepted to go to Spain in the spring with my school, but my parents refused to pay for the trip. They didn't believe it was worth it. I didn't speak to them for days. I begged and pleaded but they never relented. On my eighteenth birthday, in February, I received a letter from Quique apologizing because he had fallen in love with someone else. I felt betrayed, but only a little, because really three weeks isn't long enough for love to stick. I ended my senior year, getting into six out of the eight colleges I'd applied to, including my first-choice school, Smith College. I chose Smith because among other things, they had a very positive attitude toward studying abroad for junior year. Even though things hadn't worked out between Quique and me, my love affair with Spain was still waiting to be consummated.

5: Black Like Me

At certain times I have no race, I am me.
—ZORA NEALE HURSTON

Before I left home for college, I made a promise to myself. I absolutely, positively would not become friends with any White people. During my last two years at University School, it became increasingly clear that I had not been successful at keeping my color under wraps. Even with my hair straight and my speech generously peppered with Valley girl slang and intonations, I could not pass. The drama teacher kept offering me the "perfect roles" in the school plays, like the eye-rolling maid and the streetwise doo-wop girl, causing me to drop out of the theater scene in silent protest. The headmaster begged me to deliver Martin Luther King's "I have a dream" speech during Black History Month, because I just had a knack for "that sort of thing." That "thing," I presumed, was being colored. And when I briefly dated a boy from my Spanish class whose perfect Castilian accent gleaned from a year abroad in Spain reminded me of Quique, I upset his mother so badly she developed amnesia, never able to remember when I called or any message I left for her son.

It was high time, I reasoned, I got some Black friends and connected with the Blacker side of myself. I had half a mind to change my name to Kenyatta and wear only red, black, and green. But of course I didn't, because try as I might, I was still a Black girl who had experienced the world as a middle-class suburbanite. My formative years were spent in a preppy elitist institution and I was headed for four more as a new student at Smith College in Northampton, Massachusetts.

I chose Smith because it looked like the college of my dreams, with its redbrick buildings and manicured green lawns dotted with massive trees, well-tended gardens, and even a pond called Paradise. Smith had no official course requirements, so in my first semester I was free to take Comparative Caribbean Dance and Biology for Poets. Yes, the diversity numbers were low, comparatively speaking, but I was sure to find a whole bunch of Black girls like me who'd grown up privileged and accused of acting uppity. At the very least, I knew I wouldn't be the only Black girl in my classes anymore and I'd finally be able to embark on an authentic Negro experience of some sort.

Of course it's really hard to become authentic just like that. My roommate, Miranda, didn't help. She defined White, with her corn-silk blond hair, blue eyes, and home state of Vermont. She laughed when she recalled how her grandmother had almost had a heart attack when she found out her only granddaughter had a Negro room-mate (her words, not mine).

"There are no Black people in my town," Miranda informed me on the day we met. "But my parents are hippies and always taught us that people are the same no matter what color."

And that was that. We became friends, against my previous pledge to steer clear of the WPs. Not even twenty-four hours at Smith and I'd already fallen off the wagon.

All of the first-years (we weren't allowed to call ourselves freshmen at Smith) in my dorm were grouped together for an endless number of getting-to-know-you games, orientation meetings, and wacky practical jokes played on us by the senior class. So by the end of my first month at Smith, my new best friends all lived in my dorm and I could count the Black ones on one hand with no fingers raised. Faith was half Black, but we didn't bond. And RoseAnne, a Jamaican girl from Brooklyn, was sweet but we had nothing in common. I liked Kate from Michigan, Gail from Indiana, and Aura, who was from Ohio. Kate was white and Aura and Gail were both Asian. I felt slightly vindicated because at least I was working toward color. But back in my room, as I carefully planned out my class schedule and tried to decide what extracurriculars to pursue, I tried to get refocused on my promise to find Black girls like me. Black girls who spoke "proper," dressed preppy, and had no problem navigating mainstream culture. Black girls who listened to Top 40 radio stations and didn't necessarily know how to dance the Cabbage Patch. But they also had to know what collard greens were, didn't recoil at the thought of eating pig feet and chitterlings on special occasions, and might have one or two relatives named Boo-Boo who might or might not still be in jail. So when the invitation for the first meeting of the Black Students' Alliance arrived in my student mailbox, I felt a great sense of relief and joy. Help was on the way.

The meeting was at five o'clock. My dorm was the farthest from the center of campus where the Mwangi Cultural Center sat, so I left at four-thirty to give myself plenty of time to get there. I didn't want to miss a minute. And I went by myself. Faith wasn't interested in joining, and RoseAnne was too busy studying, but she promised she'd be at the next meeting. As I walked across campus in the setting sunlight, I couldn't help but smile. I was so happy here at Smith. I loved all of my classes. I loved the feeling of independence and freedom being so far from my family. And I loved Northampton. Whenever my friends and I had a dollar to spare, we'd head to Herrell's for pumpkin ice cream, then wander up and down Main Street peeking in the windows of all of the eclectic little shops. I had picked well. Now if I could get the Black thing going, all the pieces of the identity puzzle I was building for myself would be complete.

The Mwangi Cultural Center was actually housed in the basement of Lilly Hall, one of the oldest buildings on campus. On the outside it was redbrick and stately like most of the other Smith buildings, but inside the center there were African masks, posters of famous African Americans, and colorful swaths of African-inspired fabrics. I was early, so I looked around, admiring the plaques and photos on the walls. Only a few other girls (or rather women, as we had been instructed to refer to one another) were in the front room where chairs had been set up for the meeting. I was inexplicably nervous, like I was waiting for a blind date. Every woman/girl who walked through the door I would size up, wondering if she was going to be my new best friend. Wondering if she knew the sting of her own kind rejecting her for the way she spoke. Wondering if she was as hungry as I to find a real sister-friend who would understand the lure of pop music, Broadway show tunes, and eating really good sushi.

But nobody stopped to speak to me. Most of the women/girls seemed to know one another already. The older ones were friends from years past, and I guessed the first-years who seemed to know everyone had come to Smith early for the orientation held just for students of color. I had not attended that extra orientation because I didn't think it was necessary. I didn't need to learn how to feel comfortable living with White people. I needed prep work on dealing with my own kind.

Soon enough there was a group of girls in the room, laughing and talking, hugging and shouting. Catching up. I recognized LaTesia from the dorm attached to mine and I waved from across the room, but she was busy talking to her friends from back home in Philadelphia. They were always together. I might have imagined it, but I swore she saw me and turned away. Were they talking about me?

I sat down and waited for the meeting to come to order. I figured if I sat there and looked alone, the president or the person in charge of welcoming folks would notice me and give me a hug and draw me into the circle of women. So I plunked myself down in a brown leather swivel chair and waited for someone to come rescue me. I saw a few girls look my way and then go back to their conversations. Did I have a sign on that said Ignore Me? I felt like even though I hadn't yet opened my mouth everyone could tell I didn't belong here. I wasn't the right kind of Black girl. It was like my eighteen years of close contact with the WPs had marked me. Maybe my treachery was seeping out of my pores and creating a stinky, wet-dog smelling cloud of Whiteness over my head, making these girls tread a wide path around me. Maybe they were just waiting for me to go away so they could start. But how did they know? Had LaTesia spread the word that I had made fast friends with a lot of the White girls in my dorm? I waited five more minutes and decided I'd been marked. Before the tears already blinding my eyes could fall down my cheeks, I quietly left the building, and not one person tried to stop me.

Once outside in the cool night air, I let the tears come unheeded. I started running back to my dorm, tears flowing, snot running, feeling rejected and a loneliness so profound it blinded me. And then I tripped over a log. There on the ground in a pile of leaves I cried so hard for the Black girl inside of me who yearned to be free. I didn't know why this hurt so much. In all my years in Wisconsin, I had been happy enough and well adjusted. White people had always made up the majority of my social network and it had never really bothered me. Black people at my church, at public school, and most everywhere else in Milwaukee that wasn't dominated by my immediate family always made me feel like an interloper, so why was this rejection causing me to lose my shit in a pile of leaves? Maybe I was having a nervous breakdown. The thought of being committed to a mental institution made me wail even harder at the injustice of it all.

By the time I limped up to my room, I was still sniffling and hiccuping. I didn't think I was being loud, but the girl in the next room heard me and tapped on the door to ask if I was all right. Charlotte Park was the Korean girl from California with the boisterous laugh and colorful So-Cal wardrobe. I liked her, but we hadn't had much to talk about. Until now.

"What's the matter?" she asked me, coming into my room and making herself comfortable on the end of my bed, where I was now curled up in fetal position staring at my poster of Prince.

"I don't even know," I said between hiccups.

"Well, do you want to talk about it?" she probed.

I turned to look at Charlotte. She was really cute, with a heart-shaped face, thick shoulder-length hair, and an easy smile. She seemed genuinely interested and not like she had someplace else to be at the moment.

"I feel really stupid," I said, turning back to the wall. I didn't want to see her face when she heard my saga and decided I was a total wacko.

"Well, just tell me what happened. It's probably not that bad," she said.

And I told her. I told her how I wanted to be Black when I got to

Smith and how the BSA was supposed to be my entrée into the Black world but they had totally rejected me.

"So basically you left before the meeting even started," Charlotte commented when I finished talking.

"Yeah, I guess," I said, feeling more and more foolish as I realized how lame I sounded. I was crying and carrying on as if I'd just discovered my best friend had been killed in a horrific accident. Instead of the truth, which was that a bunch of girls ignored me at a meeting. I waited for Charlotte to make up an excuse and hightail it out of my room.

"You know what?" she said. "The girls from KASS weren't impressed with me, either. Apparently, I'm not hip enough or rich enough to be a part of their crowd. But guess what. I'm not trying only to be surrounded by other Koreans. That's not why I came to Smith. And you know what? They can kiss my ass."

I turned around again to look at this Charlotte Park. She was laughing at her own audacity.

"Really," she continued, "who needs them? Those clubs are for girls who can't deal with all this Whiteness or who want to surround themselves with only their own kind. I don't want to live like that. I never have. I'm from Orange County, where I was often the only Asian around, so like you, I don't have a problem with 'mainstream culture.' "

We both knew that "mainstream" was code for White people.

"Really?" I said, giving her my full attention. Her story was sounding a lot like my own.

"If I wanted to hang out with only Asians," Charlotte continued with her story, "I could have stayed in Cali and gone to a UC school. I came out east because I really wanted to meet different kinds of people. Especially since I'll probably end up back in California."

"Well, my roommate is as White as the folks in Wisconsin I grew up with, and I don't want or need to know more about them," I said ruefully.

"I don't think you can choose who you're going to be friends with based on their color," Charlotte said. "You're just going to be friends with whomever you have the most in common with."

"I know. You're right," I groaned. "I just had this idea that I was finally going to meet other Black girls like me here."

"You might," Charlotte said, "But it probably won't be through the BSA, it will be through a class or if you join a club or something. Just naturally."

"I know. I know," I repeated, kissing Kenyatta good-bye in my mind. And then a thought came to me. "We should start our own club, totally multi-culti and exclusive." I started to giggle.

"We should make it a token club and make sure to invite only one of every ethnic group," Charlotte offered, getting in on the joke.

"And what should our theme be?" I wondered out loud.

"Eating," Charlotte said without hesitating. I knew I liked this girl. And that was how we started Lamb Bhuna, an exclusive, multi-culti, hush-hush, affirmative-action eating club.

After the BSA fiasco, I resolved to become a multiculturalist. I would not belong to one single group (especially considering that the most obvious group to belong to didn't want me) but lay claim to all. Instead of BSA meetings, my new group of dark brown to light brown (plus Jane, our token White girl) friends and I partied with the multicultural organizations at Amherst College and the University of Massachusetts, both of which were only a short free bus ride away. I celebrated Diwali, the Hindu festival of lights, and attended Asian film screenings. I sat at the foreign language tables and tried to absorb French. I tutored a young family from Puerto Rico in English, and I had a handful of passionate and furtive flings with a random assortment of men who came to be known solely by their ethnic origins. French man. Swedish man. Jewish guy . . .

By the end of my first year at Smith, I had no idea what I was going to major in. My course load was random and wasn't helping me make a decision, although I was having tons of fun. I had started taking German classes and was pondering the possibility of going premed. My father really wanted a doctor in the family. My one class in creative writing made me rethink my secret fantasies of becoming a famous author, considering my professor gave me a C and told me I lacked

both creativity and talent. Ouch! The only steady thing in my schedule was Spanish. Even if it meant taking five academics a semester,
or waking up at 7:00 a.m. for a dreaded 8:00 a.m. class, Spanish was
fundamental to my well-being. It was my only academic constant.

Even still, I had no intention of majoring in Spanish language and
literature, which was the only option for a language major at Smith. It
was pure pleasure for me to learn to speak another language. I didn't
want it to become an obligation or a chore. And I never wanted it to
be boring, which I feared the upper-level literature classes would be.
Basically, I wanted to take Spanish classes that would allow me to play
and flirt with the language. Of course, it didn't hurt if the class was
held at UMass or Amherst, either, because then I could play and flirt
with the boys in my classes, too. So I studied political Cuban poetry
at Amherst and advanced conversation at UMass. Whenever I could,
I stopped at the Office for International Study and stared at the brochures on the wall advertising study-abroad programs in Spain. It was
too early to apply, seeing as how it was still two years away, but there
was no harm in doing some advance fantasy work.

I came back to Smith for my sophomore year with a purpose. I finally
knew what I was going to do with my life. Enough of the different major every week. No more flights of fancy. Good-bye fantasies of fortune
and fame as a writer or an actress. After spending the summer working for the city of Milwaukee at a summer enrichment program for
poor children, I realized my calling. I was meant to educate. I couldn't
wait to sign my declaration card as an education major. Working with
those poor but eager children made me realize that I had a duty to
help the less fortunate, and the schools were the best place to start.
My plan was to begin my career as a public school teacher to get ac-
quainted with the population I wanted to help. Then slowly but surely
I would work my way up to secretary of education and reform the
entire system of public education in the United States. I was so passionate about my goals, I couldn't wait to ingratiate myself with the
Education Department at Smith and get busy and get focused. Because I was a year behind, I had to make up for lost time and signed

up for three education classes each semester. I also did internships and observations at local schools and in the education department at the natural history museum back in Milwaukee.

In order to fit a year abroad in Spain into my new life plan, I had to find a program that offered classes in education. That wasn't very easy because it seemed that everyone who wanted to travel to Spain planned on majoring in Spanish, so the majority of classes fit under the language, literature, and culture category. Nobody seemed to offer courses for students like me who wanted to continue with their regular studies, but in Spanish. Like educational psychology, in Spanish. Or child development, in Spanish. The way I looked at it, becoming bilingual would make me a better teacher in the public school system, considering the growing population of Latinos (I guess my dad knew what he was talking about, after all). There had to be others like me, I reasoned, so there had to be a program out there with classes that would count toward my major.

I was lying on the floor of my dorm room, in the former maid's quarters. The room was small and hot, but it was all mine. No more roommates. Spread around me were the brochures from all of the programs that might send me to Spain. Shiny, colorful papers promising a total immersion experience, excursions throughout the Iberian Peninsula, lodging with native families or in dorms with real Spanish students. After a while, one program sounded just like the others.

"Aaaahhhh," I moaned out loud. Everyone on my hall heard me, since the door stayed open to give the illusion of space and air.

"What's the matter?" A blond freckle-faced girl named Meg popped her head in the doorway. Because she was on the swim team, she was one of the rare juniors still on campus and not studying abroad.

"I can't decide what program to apply to in Spain," I whined.

"Why aren't you going with Smith's program?" she asked.

I turned to face Meg, wondering how deeply I should go into my reasoning.

"Well, first of all," I began, "Smith doesn't offer any classes in education, and I have to be able to take at least three classes toward my major. With Smith's program you can only take classes in Spanish language, literature, and culture." I didn't also mention that as much as I loved my fellow Smithies, I didn't want to spend my year abroad surrounded by them. How would that help me immerse myself? I wanted to be as far from my real life as possible. A lot of my friends were bucking the trend and staying put at Smith for their junior year. Jane and I were the only ones in our small group going away. Jane was heading to France but had easily decided to go on Smith's program.

As I was explaining myself, two other girls had gathered around my door, India and Margaret. They were seniors who lived down the hall from me. Behind their backs I called them the Bobbsey Twins, even though India was Black and Margaret White. They did everything together, wore the same size clothing, and were always promoting some new political cause.

"Why do you want to go to Spain instead of South America?" India asked me, and I swear I heard some accusation in her tone. Like, why Europe and not a browner country? Or maybe I was imagining that. But the truth was, even some of my own family members had pressed me on this issue, wondering why I was so intent on going to a country of colonizers instead of a country where the people had been oppressed. Like oppression was a selling point.

"I've just always wanted to go to Spain," I said, hoping this wasn't going to turn into a debate. And then I added, "And I might spend the first semester in Austria because I want to practice my German, too."

"Well," India started in her best know-it-all voice, "my friend Chris went to Austria two years ago for her junior year and she said it was awful. She's Black and she said they were so racist; she had a really bad time. She was supposed to stay a year and ended up coming home after one semester."

"I've heard that about Austria, too," Margaret jumped in. "And just to add to that, everyone I knew who went abroad definitely said you should spend the entire year in one place because it takes a whole semester to get used to things and for the language to kick in."

"Yeah, I've read that, too," I admitted. The Austria idea had been a bit of a lark, but now I felt pretty sure I didn't want to go anywhere near a German-speaking country.

"So what are your choices for programs?" Meg asked. Suddenly my decision had become a group problem.

I laid out the brochures offering the three best programs, based on cost (had to be cheaper than Smith, considering university in Spain was practically free), class offerings (they had to offer something that sounded like a class in education), and housing selection (I wanted the option to live with a family or in an apartment; I didn't want to live in a dorm). Everyone agreed the Institute for European Studies presented the best options. It was half the cost of Smith and they offered financial aid. Because I could enroll directly into the University of Salamanca, where the program was based, I could take any number of education classes in their own world-famous department. And the housing options ranged from living with families to apartment living.

"I'd apply here," Margaret said, flipping through the full-color catalog. "And it says here that Smith is one of their affiliate schools, so you won't have to go through the whole process of having the program approved. That's a headache you don't want to deal with."

"What do you think, India?" I said, just wanting to hear another opinion because IES sounded too perfect and I didn't want to be sucked in by pretty pictures and easy promises.

"The way I see it, all these programs sound the same to me," India said. "Find the one that offers the classes you need and is the cheapest, and then you just have to make the most of it."

And with that Meg, India, and Margaret left my doorway, their work done, having helped an underclassman navigate her way through study abroad.

I looked at the IES brochure one more time. In Spain, my choices were Madrid and Salamanca, but only in Salamanca did the option for classes in education exist. I had never heard of the city of Salamanca, but according to the brochure it was a beautiful college town with the oldest university in Europe. I could see myself there, walking to class, speaking Spanish with all my new friends, sipping coffee in the Plaza Mayor. With a determined spirit, I gathered up all the other brochures and chucked them in the trash and filled out the application for IES, right then and there. When I was finished, I walked my application to the mail center and mailed it off. The deed was done. Finally, I was on my way.

Two weeks before my last day on campus as a sophomore I fell in deep lust. Unlike the man-boys I'd been infatuated with up until now, Craig didn't come with an accent, and his homeland was the decidedly unexotic state of Minnesota. But he was Black. Really Black. Actually his skin tone looked like burnt copper, but what he lacked in melanin, he made up for in righteousness. And he liked Me. Bourgie, Oreo, uppity me. The reason he liked me is because he recognized my inner White-girl complex. Growing up in Minnesota, he'd been cursed with the same issues. But here at Amherst, where he was already a junior, he'd reinvented himself as a Really Down Brother.

We met at one of the multi-culti parties at Amherst. The last one of the year. We danced to vintage Michael Jackson. He met my friends. We exchanged numbers. Since we had only two weeks before school ended, we knew this had to go fast. We spent every evening together, which usually meant I'd make my way over to Amherst, because a boy coming to Smith was just too obvious. When the two weeks were over, we were equally in deep like. I still couldn't believe I had captured the affections of a real Black man who didn't question my loyalty to the cause. Before we said our last good-bye, Craig promised to drive all the way to Milwaukee for the Fourth of July to visit me. Nobody had ever driven across state lines for me before.

Unfortunately, by the time the Fourth of July rolled around, all those warm fuzzy feelings about Craig had dissipated into fond memories and a lingering question as to what I had liked about him so much. But he still wanted to come, and I didn't have the heart to say no thanks. Since this was the first boy I'd ever brought home from college, my large, nosy extended family was intrigued. And this was also the weekend Miko and her family were staying with us, visiting from Arizona, where they'd moved six years ago. Needless to say, I felt a lot of pressure. I couldn't remember any of Craig's good points to share with my family except that he was really cute and had superbly toned calf muscles. I just hoped for the best, telling myself that I was a good judge of character and if I had liked the boy so much two months ago, I'd still like him when he got to my house.

"Lori, I think he's here," my mother said, peeking out the window of the living room. My heart and stomach did their own series of flip-flops and felt like they were trying to trade places. I had the ridiculous urge to run back to my room and hide, but I couldn't. Something felt wrong. We'd been having such a great time with Miko and her parents, reminiscing every night after cooking some exotic meal. I felt the love and warmth of my family so strongly, Craig's arrival felt like an intrusion. But I had invited him, so I had to make him feel welcome. I walked out to the driveway, where Craig was getting his stuff out of the car. I never thought of myself as a car snob, but when I saw Craig's rusty, beat-up, and dented Honda, I felt my nose wrinkle in distaste and felt a flash of irrational anger at him for bringing this piece of trash into my parents' yard. Horrified by my own shallow thoughts, I quickly plastered a smile on my face and wrapped my arms around Craig in a welcoming hug. He seemed overjoyed to see me.

"Wow, I'm so glad I made it," he said. "I've been driving for seven hours with no air-conditioning." That explained his powerful armpit odor, but of course I didn't say anything about that.

"Wow, what time did you leave?" I asked, resorting to small talk because his appreciative eyes all over my body were making me nervous.

"You look great," he said, and wrapped me in another hug and this time tried to kiss me. I resisted the urge to push him away and accepted his kiss with limp lips.

"Come on," I said, "come inside."

My parents had recently finished the renovations on their house and it felt modern and new. Where it had once stood as a plain, single-story ranch house, they had added an upstairs, a great room, and an expanded kitchen and front entrance. It wasn't overly large or pretentious; it felt like just the right amount of space for our family, immediate and extended. My mother's decorating style combined classic elegance with modern functionality. She liked antique furniture and French painters. Her color palette began and ended with shades of pale pink and deep greens. Our houses were never cozy like my aunt Minerva's, but they were always the best place to have a big family gathering. Craig was not impressed. In fact, as I showed him around the house, including where he'd be sleeping, in my pink room, his one observation was that our house seemed cold.

After that, things just went downhill. Craig refused to eat Miko's mother's Asian noodle dish for dinner that night, read the paper at the breakfast table the following morning, completely ignoring the rest of us, and somehow managed to maintain the same level of arm-pit odor he'd arrived with, despite showering.

"He seems angry or something," my little brother whispered to me in confidence after breakfast. "And he's got some powerful body odor. I almost fainted when he was playing baseball with me outside." I knew I should reprimand Lee and stick up for Craig, but I didn't know what was wrong with him. What had I done to warrant these bad manners?

Sunday morning we finally understood what we had done wrong. We were eating breakfast and my sister asked Craig to please pass the bread basket.

"You don't have to say please," he said, barely masking his contempt.

"I'm sorry?" she asked.

"Yeah, you guys say please and thank you so much, like you're putting on airs. It's just us here. Why the fake formality?"

My sister was insulted. "What's wrong with saying please and thank you? I don't call that formality, I call it being polite."

"You guys just sound so, White."

He said it.

I couldn't take it anymore. "What are you talking about?" I practically yelled.

Craig didn't yell back. In fact he was very much under control when he responded. It was like he'd been rehearsing this speech for years, just waiting for the right family to unleash his opinions on.

"It's just so phony the way you please and thank you all the time in some sort of mimicry of White European culture."

My sister couldn't believe this. "Oh, so saying please and thank you is only something White people can say? That is so ridiculous. Mom, isn't that ridiculous?

My mother, probably wondering by this time why I had brought this angry Black man into her house, decided to try to keep the peace.

"Well, maybe Craig was brought up differently," my mother said, directing her comments to my sister. "So this may seem false to him." Then she turned to Craig and said, "But perhaps what you're witnessing is something more native to the region. Here in the Midwest we are known for being overly polite. It's true. So maybe your observation has less to do with race and more to do with where you're from."

I thought that sounded diplomatic and maybe even kind of true.

Craig just rolled his eyes. We all finished our breakfast in silence. Craig quickly excused himself and returned to his/my room.

Ten minutes later we heard the front door slam and a car start.

"Is he leaving?" I said to no one in particular. Craig was supposed to stay one more night. I jumped up and ran back to my room. Sure enough, his stuff was gone and there was a note on a small piece of yellow paper. I picked up the note without reading it and ran back to the dining room to announce the good news.

"He's gone!" And then I added as an afterthought, "He didn't even say good-bye. Should I be mad?"

"Are you mad?" Miko asked.

I didn't even have to think about that. "No way."

A collective sigh went around the table. There was a moment of silence as everyone tried to collect their thoughts about Craig and tried to decide if they should say anything or nothing. My sister broke the silence.

"I'm sorry, Lori, but he was a real jerk."

"And he smelled bad," my brother added, as if I needed reminding. My whole bedroom smelled like a giant, funky armpit.

"Lee," my father intervened. "That is not necessary."

"He did have an odor problem," my mother said, sticking up for her son.

"What exactly was it that you saw in him, Lori?" Miko asked.

I felt so embarrassed and upset that I had subjected my friends and family to the poison of Craig. I don't know what I had seen in him. Black pride? Acceptance? My shot at an authentic Negro experience? Now everyone must think I had no standards and that I picked up wacky guys. Great.

I offered Miko a lame excuse and hoped everyone would give me one freebie as boys go. "He seemed really great back at Amherst when I met him," I said.

Miko's father, Tim, always the voice of reason, finished the conversation. "Well, he's gone now. Let's just enjoy the rest of the weekend."

And that's exactly what we did.

6: Dreaming *en Español*

I hate to fly. Ever since that horrific Pan Am flight blew up over Scotland in 1988, I've been that person on the plane moving her lips in a nonstop silent prayer in an effort to keep the giant metal bird in the air. Once I'm on the plane, I spend the entire time wishing I wasn't on the plane. Sweating. Trying not to hyperventilate. Averting my eyes from the window in case the wing is on fire or about to fall off.

On September 8, 1992, I was on a plane flying over the Atlantic Ocean. And even though it wasn't my first transatlantic flight, it was my first transatlantic flight alone. I managed to unfurl my fingers from around the armrest and unclench my eyes about two hours into the trip by concentrating on my final destination and listening intently to Michael Jackson tell me how "bad" he was on his latest album. I was about to come face-to-face with my destiny. In my secret heart of hearts I truly believed that something was going to change my life forever in Spain. I didn't have a concrete vision, just a feeling, or maybe it was a hope that I would find the real me in Spain. Something about the way Quique had loved me made me hopeful that the place that created him would understand me.

Somewhere in the middle of the ocean I fell asleep.

When I woke up, the sun was shining through the cracks of the airplane windows. People were beginning to move around in their seats and unwrap themselves from their homemade cocoons. I was sitting in the middle of the plane and I could hear the stewardesses beginning their rounds of breakfast service in the back rows. I read somewhere that most airplane crashes occur within twenty minutes of takeoff, so by hour six of the ride, I was as relaxed as I was going to get. And with landing in the imminent future I was downright giddy. I stopped bouncing in my seat only by reminding myself that bouncing couldn't possibly be good for the plane's equilibrium when we were still flying over water.

I looked around me to see if anyone nearby looked like they too were as excited as I and might want to talk. Maybe another student on his way for a junior year abroad. I noticed a boy across the aisle who looked vaguely familiar. Was that just my overeager imagination, or was it possible to bump into someone you know 150,000 feet up in the air?

With nothing to lose I cleared my throat. "Excuse me, what's your name? You look really familiar," I started, cringing at the way I sounded, like I was trying to pick up a cute boy at a frat party.

"David," he said, looking at me as if I wasn't so familiar. Probably trying to figure out where he might know a Black girl with a voice that sounded too much like Minnie Mouse crossed with a midwestern Valley girl to be for real.

David. I knew a lot of Davids. I needed more.

"What's your last name?" I tried.

"Johnson," he said with a kind of guarded neutrality that didn't say leave me alone, but wasn't exactly a suggestion to continue with my interrogation.

When you're on an airplane that originated in New York City, is bound for Spain, you're coming from college in Massachusetts, but you live in Milwaukee, the possibilities are endless as to where you might know David from. But I didn't have anything else pressing. Breakfast was still several seats back.

I started with my most recent reality. Smith. Seeing how Smith is a women's college, I might know David from the greater Pioneer Valley. "Do you go to Amherst or UMass?" I asked. He said no. He went to school in the Midwest. So I redirected to my hometown. "Are you from Milwaukee?" I asked. He said yes. Now we were getting somewhere.

"Wait a minute. Did you go to Atwater?" he asked me, suddenly getting animated.

"Yeah, but just for a year," I said, recalling my exile from private school.

"Right, you were in my sixth-grade class," David said, giving me his first genuine grin. He turned toward me in his seat and we started talking for real. He caught me up on the lives of my sixth-grade classmates, the ones I remembered and those I didn't. I barely remembered David, except that he was a nice boy in my homeroom class. He was still nice. Turned out David was heading to Spain for his junior year, too, except he was only staying for a semester. Still, it was reassuring to know that someone from my own hometown would be in the same country.

"What city are you going to?" I asked.

"Seville," David said, pronouncing it, I noticed, like an American. "What about you?"

"I'm going to Salamanca," I said, already sad that my new old friend and I wouldn't have a chance to get reacquainted.

"Where's Salamanca? I've never heard of it," David said.

"It's a small college town like ninety miles northwest of Madrid. Like the distance between Milwaukee and Chicago," I said, putting it into familiar terms. I still didn't really know much about Salamanca, either. I knew it was famous for its ancient university, but I couldn't find anyone who had actually been there to color in the details. Even Señora Spector, who had since fled the United States and moved to Madrid, had never been to the "famous" college town.

"Cool. Maybe I can come visit sometime," David said with that easy familiarity young travelers get when they leave home. Friendships are sudden and intense until you get back to the USA, where emotions are checked and intimacy is reserved for the bedroom.

"Great," I said, happy to have the comfort of this familiar.

By the time breakfast arrived, David and I had run out of things to say to each other and we got engrossed in our cold, doughy rolls and watery orange juice so that we could end the conversation without saying so.

"Ladies and gentlemen, we will be landing in Madrid in approximately thirty minutes," the pilot announced. First in English and then in Spanish.

I closed my eyes and leaned back in my seat with a smile on my face. A new chapter was about to begin in my life story.

• • •

It's hard to tell anything about a country by its international airport. At Madrid's Barajas Airport, the first thing I noticed that was different was the smoke. It made my eyes sting and my lungs ache. Everyone around me seemed to be smoking cigarettes as they ambled through customs and then stood in front of one of the three baggage carousels, waiting for their suitcases. Aside from the smoky stench, Spain didn't feel as foreign as Morocco had. A lot of people were even speaking English. There were White people, Black Africans, Asians, and ambiguous brown people all around me doing their own thing. I did notice that everyone, save the conspicuous American students like myself, seemed rather well dressed.

Before I left the United States, I had received a letter telling me to take a taxi from the airport to a downtown Madrid location where the official IES welcoming orientation would be held. The Institute for European Studies didn't collect their students at the airport, like the AFS directors had in Morocco. I was a college student now, so I guess that meant I was old enough to fend for myself in a foreign country. I suppose somebody had decided that twenty-year-old American students should be able to navigate airports, taxis, and crippling jet lag. Upon entering the bustling lobby of the airport, where everyone seemed to be trying to get somewhere else, I experienced a moment of panic and doubt that perhaps I wasn't old enough. But then I realized I didn't have much of a choice, so I called on my "I Am Woman Hear Me Roar" inner Smithie and held my bags a little tighter and followed the signs for taxis. Thank God the word "taxi" is the same in English and Spanish.

By the time my taxi driver pulled up in front of the anonymous building, I was sweating profusely. It was still really hot in Madrid in September, and the entire ride there I was wondering if my grammatically correct but poorly accented Spanish had been understood when I gave the driver the address. I was sure I smelled pretty bad, too, considering I'd been wearing the same clothes for more than sixteen hours by then. A middle-aged man in a brown suit that looked entirely too hot for the day's weather was standing on the steps of the building with a name tag that read "Daniel Pastor, Director IES." He wasn't sweating.

As I opened the door of the taxi, I was so relieved.

"Yeah, I made it," I announced, struggling with my giant green backpack, purse, and secret money belt. Thankfully the driver immediately popped the trunk, because I couldn't remember how to say "trunk" in Spanish at that moment.

"Bienvenida. Tú tienes que ser Lori," Daniel Pastor said to me.

"Wow, you're good," I said, wondering if he had memorized all of the photos we had sent in as part of the application process.

I dragged my suitcase out of the trunk while Sr. Pastor watched calmly, not offering to help. I paid the driver what seemed like a whole lot of pesetas and he sped off.

With all of my earthly possessions for the next nine months spread around me, and still sweating like a pig, I looked at Daniel and waited for some words of encouragement, welcome, or maybe even a hug. What I got instead was a rapid-fire list of instructions in Spanish.

I smiled one of my best smiles and replied, "I'm sorry, I'm so tired and out of it. Can you please speak to me in English? I swear I'll be ready to speak Spanish by tomorrow."

Daniel Pastor gave me a look that seemed to say, "Oh, you poor stupid American, this is going to be harder on me than on you." Then he proceeded to repeat himself in Spanish, only a tad slower. I tried really hard to understand what he was saying but only managed to pull out a word here and there. One of them sounded like "upstairs." So in two trips I dragged my luggage up the steps of the building, found an elevator, and thankfully found signs that said IES, indicating that we were meeting on the fifth floor.

When I reached the fifth floor, I found a room packed with other students like myself. I looked around at the crowd and felt immediately overwhelmed and alone. Before the tears that were starting to form behind my eyelids had a chance to fall, a short, chubby Black girl with thick braids came bounding over to me.

"You must be Lori," she said.

"Yeah, how'd you know?" I asked. She gave me a knowing smile and said, "Because I got here an hour ago and all the IES people were calling me Lori."

"Oh," I said, scanning the room for other Black or brown faces, and finding none, realized why Daniel Pastor knew exactly who I was. Cold panic crept into my heart and spread up to my throat, where it stayed lodged. Had I made a mistake? Was being Black going to be a liability here in Spain? Truth was, I'd never really bothered to research racial attitudes in Spain when I was busy dreaming of my arrival on the Iberian Peninsula. I just assumed the Spaniards would be as welcoming to me as the French had been to Josephine. The Spaniards who'd come to my high school seemed cool with Black people. More than cool. They seemed genuinely color blind, without a hint or suggestion that they placed some qualifier on skin color. Should I have stayed at Smith with my friends? I could be in my dorm right now eating Domino's pizza and Buffalo wings and watching *Dirty Dancing* on tape with my girls. I felt my eyes misting up in front of this girl whose name I hadn't even bothered to ask.

"What's your name?" I managed through my growing despair.

"Hilary," she said. "And yes, we're the only ones here. I checked. And we're both going to Salamanca," she added. "We're probably going to start a riot out there," she said, laughing.

I didn't know what to say. I was processing all of this information. Still thinking about Buffalo wings in the back of my mind, wondering if it was too late to stay for only one semester instead of a year, when Daniel Pastor came into the room.

"Bienvenidos todos," he began and the room fell silent. There were probably fifty of us twenty-year-olds packed into that room. Some of them, I found out later, came from the same school, so they knew one another. There was like an entire contingent of Gap-clad girls from Tufts University. Others, like me, were flying solo. Why had I been so freaking eager to be independent?

As he had downstairs with me, Daniel refused to speak English, but he spoke really slowly and gestured a lot with his hands. All around me I noticed that a lot of people seemed as confused and out of sorts as I, and that gave me comfort. By the end of the speech I had surmised that we were supposed to pick up a welcome packet and then we were going to the place where we would be staying for our ten-day orientation in Madrid.

Getting the packet was easy enough, but I had no idea what to do next. I tried to ask one of the women sitting at the information table for help in English, but it was like she had taken a solemn oath to speak only Spanish to us. At this point I didn't appreciate their commitment to our language learning. In a brochure "total immersion" sounds like a really commendable concept for those of us who really want to master the language. But in reality, being forced to speak Spanish is as enjoyable as being forced to eat liver. You know it's good for you but you're still tempted to bite the hand that's putting it on your plate. Was I the only one who felt it was more important that we be given instructions in our native language rather than using this as an opportunity to make sure we knew how to conjugate the imperfect tense? There were men in green uniforms with guns patrolling the streets as we came in from the airports. Surely there were some safety issues we should be briefed on, right? My concerns apparently were my own, as everybody else began to fan out across the room, collect their belongings, and head for the stairs. I wasn't clear on what was I supposed to do exactly, but I knew I didn't want to do it alone.

Hilary didn't speak or understand Spanish any better than I, but she was much better at survival techniques. She found a guy named Rosario from California who was practically bilingual and was working at being his best friend. I in turn stuck to Hilary like a lifeline. Eventually, after another taxi ride, we ended up at el Colegio Mayor Universitario de San Agustín, which was an all-male dormitory for a nearby college. I found my room on the third floor, down a long hallway with single rooms reserved for all of us IES students. I said goodbye to Hilary, flopped down on my bed, and cried myself to sleep.

When I woke up, it was morning.

I am in Spain. This was my first thought. I didn't move. I lay in my bed and tried to feel Spain. Did I feel any different? A wave of embarrassment washed over me as I remembered my frustrations of the day before. In the immortal words of my fellow Milwaukeeans, Laverne and Shirley, I was making my dreams come true, yet I cried so much you'd think I was here against my will. I gave myself a pep talk. "Lori, you are here for only nine months. You'd better take advantage of every single moment because it'll be over before you know it. And besides, you've wanted this forever, so get out there and immerse yourself in Spain. Go have your adventure. Go meet your destiny!"

My destiny had to wait until after I ate my breakfast. I followed my nose down to the cafeteria, where I found a lot of Spanish boys in T-shirts, sweatpants, and Adidas flip-flops alongside my fellow Americans, breaking bread together. Actually it was just like an American high school cafeteria. The Spaniards sat together and the Americans sat together. There was no mingling. And why should there be? This was just a pit stop for most of us until we were placed in our permanent homes. It seemed that about three-quarters of the people I had seen yesterday would be staying here in Madrid, while only fifteen of us would be heading to Salamanca at the end of orientation. And of those fifteen, only a handful of us planned on staying the entire year.

I found a table with three other girls. I didn't see Hilary. Two of them went to Tufts together, and one girl went to a school I had never heard of somewhere in the South. Over bread, chocolate milk, butter, and Oscar Meyer ham we quickly shared our life stories. We didn't really have anything in common, but I wasn't about to get picky with anyone who willingly spoke English.

"Have you met your roommate yet?" one girl asked me.

"No," I said. "I only know her name is Kristy."

"Oh, I think I met her yesterday," said one of the Tufts girls, with a look to her friend that I interpreted to mean "poor Lori." Before I had a chance to ask about Kristy, I felt a tap on my shoulder.

"Haaaiii. Are you Lori?"

I turned around to find a plump, pale White girl with long sandy blond hair, a wife-beater, cut-off denim shorts, and rubber flip-flop sandals. She had a thin braid on the side of her head that she had secured with a red rubber band. She spoke with a pronounced Texas twang and had a ready smile.

"Yes, I'm Lori," I said while trying really hard not to fixate on the fact that the girl's breasts were far too big for her to be walking around with just a man's undershirt on in a cafeteria full of Spanish men.

"Hi, roomie," she said then, and I understood the Tufts girl's look. Kristy just gave off the vibe of "interesting character," which no doubt translated to "bad roommate."

Without prompting, Kristy gave me an abbreviated version of her life and mission for her year abroad (she was one of the handful who would be staying). Since she was from Texas she was already very comfortable with Spanish, but she wanted to be totally fluent by the time she left so she was not going to speak a word of English. And she was going to see to it that I didn't, either. She ended her little speech with a "We're going to have such a good time. Bye." And with a perky little wave she was off.

I tried to remain positive. Maybe under all that 1970s hair, Kristy and I would find some common interests. I smiled at my tablemates and they just shook their heads and gave me looks of such pity, I had to laugh.

They didn't know I was the queen of making friends with people who don't look like me and don't come from the same place as me. Kristy and I would be fine. Besides, I wasn't here to become best buds with American girls. I wanted to experience the culture and the people of Spain. It was better to do that without being too connected to other Americans. They would just be distractions. Even though in my regular life back home I was very rarely without my group of girlfriends, I had psyched myself up to be lonely for this year abroad in the name of having a more meaningful experience. It was poetic, I thought. And I believed I had the soul of a poet.

Nine days later I was on a bus to Salamanca. "*Es preciosa,*" María, one of the IES guides, was telling me. Precious? I thought. Salamanca is precious? What was that supposed to mean? I thought, gnashing my teeth. I was getting a bit worried. It seemed that every time I asked someone about Salamanca, "*preciosa*" was the adjective used to describe it. For some reason I assumed "*preciosa*" might be a euphemism for something not so good, like "charming" means cramped and crusty when describing real estate in New York City.

The truth of the matter was that the last ten days in Madrid had been the best days of my life. Madrid was perfect. It was old but stately. Full of history and elegance. Bustling with activity but at a pace that allowed for strolling and sipping strong coffee while watching time pass by. Every day began with an organized trip to a museum or a castle, and every night, my new posse of friends and I headed out to the clubs and bars to dance to techno beats and drink free-flowing, watered-down sangria. Always the teetotaler back home due to a doctor's warning that alcohol could diminish the effects of the anti-seizure medication I'd been taking since I was thirteen, in Spain I decided to test the doctor's warnings by happily slurping down the national party drink as well as a few mixed drinks here and there. But it wasn't the alcohol that made me so happy. It was the feeling of complete and total liberation. I was free to do whatever I wanted. Staying out at night. Sleeping all morning. Flirting shamelessly with the boy down the hall in the dormitory who seemed to enjoy immensely my shock and feigned horror at seeing his purple underwear when he dropped his pants for the fun of it at random times in a conversation. I hadn't acted like this in Morocco. Or when I had gone away to camp in Massachusetts back in high school. It wasn't just being away from home.

Something about the air in Madrid made me lose my inhibitions and fears and desires to be safe. Walking past the beautiful Parque del Retiro at night, I'd see young people on the park benches kissing each other as if their lives depended on it, not caring who witnessed their passion and desire. At first I turned away, embarrassed, but as the days passed, I grew emboldened by these public displays of emotion and sensuality. People here, it seemed, were free to follow their hearts. And with that freedom I felt the weight of race removed from my burdened shoulders. The rules of who I was supposed to be as a Black girl in America didn't count in Spain. I could talk White and listen to Céline Dion without repercussions from the Are You Black Enough? police. I could expose the sensual, foulmouthed, arrogant side of myself without fear of censure from the White People in Charge. I felt like I might be able to introduce myself without having to start the conversation with the color of my skin.

Back to the bus ride to Salamanca. It seemed that none of the

Spanish college students paid by IES to escort us to Salamanca knew anything about the place.

"Is it like Segovia?" I asked, hoping they could at least compare it to one of the cities we had just visited on our little day trips.

"*Sí, un poquito,*" the guy named Antonio said.

"Is it more like Toledo?" I tried.

"*Sí, un poquito,*" Antonio answered, nodding in agreement.

This wasn't helping.

I looked around the bus. Nobody else seemed as agitated as I about what we were about to encounter. In fact, in the fifteen of us heading to the place with no description, the only emotion that seemed to register on anyone's face was boredom. As I looked at my fellow IESers, I decided that as a group we looked like the leftovers. There was the boy with the purple underwear, my roommate Kristy, four kids from that school I never heard of in the South who all spoke with painfully strong southern accents in English and Spanish, two girls who looked way more mature than I ever felt and kept to themselves, Hilary, and a handful of Tufts coeds who were staying for only one semester. I chided myself then for being so judgmental—a trait I was actively trying to get rid of in my personality. Give love, get love, I reminded myself.

Using meditation techniques I'd learned in a Kabuki theater class I took during my "I'm going to be a famous actress" phase, I gave up my mission to deconstruct Salamanca and sat back down in my seat and tried to relax and enjoy the journey. I tried to remember the lessons I had learned in Morocco about all answers coming with time. But it was so hard because I already missed the friends I'd made during orientation. Why were they all staying in Madrid? Christina and Dagmar had begged me on the last night to ask Daniel Pastor if it was too late to switch to Madrid, but I had said no, believing I was meant to go to Salamanca for a reason. Besides, I always regretted last-minute decisions.

7: Sally

Salamanca wasn't precious, it was pink. Actually, it was more salmon colored. Everything. The buildings, the cobblestones, the benches and stairs in the quad at the university. Very monochrome. I didn't like it. I like color, lots of it. And palm trees if possible. Salamanca didn't have much vegetation of any kind. I couldn't help but compare sleepy Salamanca to the vibrancy of Madrid, and even with the oldest university in Europe, Salamanca couldn't compete in my mind.

When we arrived, we came in the back way, past the bus station and the cemetery. Our host families met the bus, lined up on the sidewalk looking neither pleased nor excited to meet their new American students. Here I was, waiting for the warm embrace of a Spanish family looking to expand their knowledge of the big wide world, when in fact, most of the stern-looking women here to collect their American guests were taking in students as a way to support themselves as divorcées, widows, or (gasp) women who had never married.

Hermi was a new divorcée with two teenagers. Her once spacious apartment had now become a crowded boardinghouse for an international group of students. With Kristy and me the number of students climbed to five, seven if you counted Hermi's own kids, Julián and María. Hermi herself was a nervous ball of chain-smoking energy who didn't think twice about taking off her bedroom *zapatilla* (slipper) to beat Julián for some infraction or another. Even though he did make his mother's life more difficult than necessary, I still felt bad for him. I mean, what teenage boy wants to share a room with his mother and sister so some *"guiris"* (that's Spanish for "damn foreigners") could have his old room?

Hermi walked us back to her house, Kristy and I dragging our heavy suitcases behind us, without saying much during the entire twenty-five-minute journey. When we got to the apartment, she gave us a quick tour, bypassing the room she shared with her kids, and laid out the rules. The hot water was to be used sparingly and not after 10:00 p.m. Mealtimes were a family affair, meaning be here on time or you won't eat. And most important, absolutely no English would be tolerated in the house. She made it sound like she was only reinforcing what Daniel Pastor had told her, but I got the sneaking suspicion that she didn't want us speaking English because she couldn't understand it herself. The rules explained, Hermi left Kristy and me to unpack.

Our room was small. The two twin beds and the armoire squashed in between left little room for anything else. I left half of my clothes in the suitcase and shoved it under my bed, stored the other half of my clothes in my side of the armoire, and then tried to decide if I should hang up the few pictures of my friends and family I had brought from home. I turned to Kristy to see what she thought and found her dusting off a photograph in a silver frame of a guy with red hair and a huge smile. My mind immediately flashed on a memory of Howdy Doody.

"This is my boyfriend, Wayne," Kristy said, before I had a chance to ask.

"Oh, he looks nice," I said, trying to suppress the urge to say something snarky. I had a thing about girls who showcased their boyfriends as if it validated their existence or something. That was a by-product of going to a fierce women's college and growing up as the girl on the dance floor dancing with herself.

Kristy took another picture out of her suitcase. It was another picture of Wayne. This one was a headshot.

One more Wayne photo came out of the bag and settled on the table next to Kristy's bed, where she could kiss his frozen visage every night before she fell asleep. As if on cue, Hermi popped her head in the room just then to give Kristy a package that had arrived in the mail that morning. It was from Wayne. Unbelievable.

"Ohhh," Kristy squealed. "He's so sweet. He promised to send me a cassette tape every week so I wouldn't forget his voice."

I tried to hold in the sarcastic comment about what kind of guy takes the time to make tapes for his girlfriend. I wouldn't be rude. I was probably just jealous.

"Wow, he sounds committed," I said, hoping that sounded like a compliment.

Hermi poked her head in the room again, this time wagging her finger at us as she reminded us that in her house *sólo español*.

I turned to Kristy. "Do you think she was eavesdropping?" I said.

"*No sé*," Kristy responded in Spanish.

"You know we don't have to speak in Spanish if we don't want to. I mean, why would we speak to each other in Spanish when we both speak English? I mean, that's kind of dumb, isn't it?" I said to Kristy, hoping she'd see the uselessness of two American girls stumbling through a conversation in Spanish. But she didn't.

"*Tenemos que hablar en español, Lori*," she said. "Otherwise how are you going to learn to speak any better?"

That sounded like an insult. And I knew I did in fact need to practice—a lot—but that didn't mean I wanted to hear it from my over-eager, Wayne-loving roommate.

Once classes started in October, my days followed a predictable rhythm. I had passed the language requirement to register for classes at the famed Universidad de Salamanca, so I was taking two classes with Spaniards, and my other three courses I took with my fellow American IES students. Unlike in the States, where courses ran on the semester, in Spain each university class lasted the entire academic year. For my education requirement, I signed up for a class called Comparative Education. Daniel Pastor warned me that the professor was very strict and serious but a very important woman in the world of pedagogy. For my other class at the university, I signed up for German.

Back at Smith, I would be starting German III, so I signed up for what seemed to be the equivalent level in Salamanca. The first day of class I realized that my enthusiastic attitude but poor study habits hadn't prepared me to take German III in Spain, where I'd be forced to translate from German to English and then Spanish. My head hurt after ten minutes of exercises. Immediately after class, I went to the registrar and downgraded myself to German II.

◊   ◊   ◊   ◊

"I'm in love," I announced to nobody and everybody in the dining room. Despite the fact that it was Wednesday, which meant garbanzo beans and pig fat in chicken broth for lunch, I was giddy. At the lunch table that day everyone was accounted for. There were no empty spaces. It was me and Kristy, Hermi and her children, another American girl, a French girl, and a Spanish boy named Miguel. Even with this many people, Hermi tried to give us all personal attention.

"So what's his name?" Hermi asked me, dragging on a cigarette. She rarely ate, choosing to smoke at the table and make sure we all appreciated her cooking.

"I don't know," I said, staring into my bowl, trying to see how much pig fat I had been awarded this day.

"Where does he live?" she tried again.

"I don't know," I said, picking around the fat to get to the beans and few noodles floating in the broth.

"*¿Es guapo?*" she asked. Is he good looking? Finally, something I could answer.

"He's so cute," I said, using the word I hoped you're supposed to use for cute boys and not for babies or small furry animals. There is a difference in Spanish.

"So, are you going to go out with him?" Kristy asked, cutting to the chase.

Now, how could I answer that when I didn't even know the boy's name? "I just saw him today in my German class," I started to explain. He came to class wearing a gray Rutgers sweatshirt that caught my eye. Like almost every Spanish boy I had seen so far, he had brown hair and dark eyes, but his hair was kind of wild and curly. His features were chiseled perfection, and he had perfectly straight white teeth, which I had noticed was an anomaly in Spain. I often found myself recoiling in horror when people bared their crooked yellow teeth in a friendly smile.

As a proud Smith College student I hated to admit that a cute boy was bringing me out of the doldrums to which I had sunk since arriving in Salamanca. But it was true.

It had been a month and I still felt like I had those first two weeks in Casablanca. Alone, isolated, and uninspired to do anything about it. I hadn't anticipated feeling culture shock in a Western European country, so it hit me that much harder. Most of the other Americans in my program didn't seem to share my problem. Every weekend, meaning Thursday through Sunday, they'd be found at the same bar, El Skud, chugging beers with other Americans, thoroughly enjoying the unlimited access to alcohol and all-night carousing. Maybe because they were going home after the first semester, they didn't feel the need to change their habits. Me, I wanted to change immediately. I wanted to *be* Spanish for the entire year but didn't know where to begin. The Spaniards in my classes, who I thought would become my tour guides into *la vida española*, didn't even seem to notice me, much less attempt to be my friend. I entered and exited my two classes at the university with about as much fanfare as a dust bunny. The Spanish students in Salamanca were so used to foreigners, if not a bit tired of them, that my adorable American face meant nothing. So Cute Boy in my German class suddenly gave me something to get excited about. I could feel my feminist card being revoked, but I didn't care. I spent hours trying to figure out what his name might be, how he got that Rutgers sweatshirt, and if he'd have a problem falling madly in love with a Black American girl.

Before I left Smith, I had promised myself that I was not going to get attached to any boys because that would surely end in heartbreak. Anything that started in Spain would have to end there because I didn't believe in long-distance romance. And why even go there when you knew ahead of time how it was going to end? Given my current circumstances, plagued as I was with crippling culture shock, I decided a healthy crush would be allowed. If nothing else, I could be flexible.

Having hidden my pig fat and the rest of my garbanzo beans under my napkin, I announced, *"He terminado."* I'm done. "Excuse me." I left the table and went to wash up. I planned to spend the three droopy hours of siesta parked in the Plaza Mayor waiting for Cute Boy to walk by. You never know, it could happen.

It was only the middle of October, and already my journal pages were filled with poems expressing my loneliness and despair.

> I was far from home
> I was all alone
> I was looking for the place that I could call my own
>
> I had left behind
> What I could call mine
> I was searching for that something that I could not find.

For some reason, the Spanish concept of *mañana, mañana, ma-ñana* left me feeling aimless and un-put-together. For the first time in my life it really didn't matter what I did with myself all day. I didn't have to go to class because my grades weren't going to transfer back to Smith, only my credits. I didn't belong to any club or organization that demanded my attention or active participation. And I didn't have any friends who counted on my companionship. Except for tutoring my German professor's son in English once a week, there seemed to be no real purpose to my life in Spain. I kept asking myself why I was here and what was I supposed to be accomplishing. I was so used to being busy and overextended and on a mission that this siesta-loving lifestyle threw me. And the worst part was, I didn't have anyone to talk to to help me sort out my confusion. I tried to coordinate phone calls back home to my friends in the States, but since I had to call on a pay phone from the street, usually in the middle of the night to catch them at home, that didn't turn out to be a satisfactory solution. Thank God I met Brook.

Brook and I first met in the Plaza de Anaya in front of the university, soon after I arrived in Salamanca. She approached me to ask for help finding a building. Judging by her utilitarian jeans, rosebud-speckled long underwear worn as a shirt, pale skin, and unstyled long brown hair, I assumed she was an American. After talking to Brook for just a few minutes I recognized a kindred spirit. Brook was from Indiana, was only eighteen, and had come to Salamanca by herself to learn Spanish. No program. No itinerary. Just a ticket and a positive attitude. She was an adventurer, a traveler, and a language enthusiast. Things I wanted to be myself but so far hadn't quite figured out how.

First Brook and I were just plaza buddies, meeting in the Plaza Mayor occasionally to go for walks, try tapas places together, and just talk. In one of our marathon conversations, she explained how she had grown into this brave person with a traveler's spirit in South Bend, Indiana. "My mother was a professor and she always had this international group of friends over to the house," Brook explained. "We even hosted foreign graduate students, so I guess I've always been comfortable around different kinds of people," she said, shrugging her slim shoulders. It was true, with Brook I really felt like I could be myself, comfortable in my own skin. What's more, she was always up to any adventure or kooky idea I wanted to try to "experience the Spanish lifestyle," like trekking all over Salamanca to try to find a hole-in-the-wall chicken joint where I heard all the college students went for the best rotisserie chicken and fried potatoes at bargain-basement prices.

Brook was fast becoming a real friend, but she had her own life to tend to that didn't always include me and my adventures. I turned to writing to chronicle my growing frustration and depression. On the pages of my journal I tried to give myself permission to feel lonely. That was normal, I reasoned. But I still felt guilty for not being able to take advantage of my dream come true. So finally, I decided to take drastic action. I couldn't stand my own aimless grief any longer.

On a Saturday afternoon, after stopping for my requisite apple tart and devouring it in the Plaza Mayor, I headed to a small shop off the plaza. I had noticed it a couple of times on my way home from class. I did not hesitate but walked right in and with my best Spanish accent said, "I'd like to buy a guitar." I figured if I was going to spend my time feeling blue and writing bad poetry, I might as well put a sound track to my misery and perhaps channel all my pain into a career as a street performer. Didn't all great music come from a place of pain? Every night the plaza filled up with wannabe rock stars on their guitars and harmonicas, playing for money. Some of them were really good and some were really awful, but they all made me think I could do that and use my loneliness for a greater purpose. I've always envisioned myself as a performer; I just lacked the instrument. So with a guitar and my heart full of pain, I might just become the next Tracy Chapman. Of course, I had to find a teacher first.

Based entirely on stereotypes, I reasoned that finding a guitar teacher in Spain should be as easy as finding an aspiring actress in Los Angeles. And I was right. I plucked the first sign I saw advertising guitar lessons from a bulletin board near the university. The photocopied piece of paper said simply "Guitar: classical, pop, rock" and three things I couldn't translate. And there was a phone number. I ripped the sign off the wall and called the number from a pay phone near Hermi's house.

A man answered on the first ring. I hadn't thought this through, but I managed to stammer out my desire for guitar lessons. The guy's name was Pablo and he gave me his address and we made an appointment for the following Monday. I made him repeat his address three times to make sure I had written it down correctly. When I got home, I grabbed my guitar out of my room and headed to the empty room recently vacated by Kristina from California. Hermi wouldn't let me take the room because she wanted another paying boarder, but since it was currently empty, I reasoned it would be okay to use it for practice space. I pulled my beautiful Spanish guitar out of its soft case and delicately strummed my fingers along the strings. I did that for a while, imagining myself playing tortured songs to a captive audience in one of the many clubs here in Salamanca. (I had already upgraded my fantasy from street performer to lounge act.) And then it hit me. I had just made an appointment with some random guy whose name I found on a flyer. What was I thinking? I'd never be so careless back

home in America. The old me would have looked up a local conserva-
tory or headed to the music department at the college and found a
recommendation for a reputable guitar instructor. But I wasn't home.
And my life wasn't like anything I recognized. So I squashed any mis-
givings and concentrated on the visions of myself playing the guitar
so passionately my fingers would bleed and people would be moved
to tears. I fell asleep to the sound of my own applause.

On Monday after class I grabbed a map from a local *librería*, found
the street Pablo lived on, and started walking. He told me it was far
from the city center. Close to the bullring, which I knew to be on the
very outskirts of town. I had walked that far only once. But since time
was always on my side in Salamanca, I didn't worry about how long it
would take. I just walked. As I was walking I tried to clarify for myself
what I wanted Pablo to teach me. I decided since I was in Spain, taking lessons from a Spanish guitar teacher, I ought to request lessons
in classic Spanish guitar picking and playing. I mean, why bother
otherwise? I didn't allow myself to consider any sinister plans Pablo
might have regarding my person.

When I finally reached Pablo's apartment building about an hour
later, I was nervous, excited, and tired. I announced my arrival in the
doorbell intercom and he buzzed me up. Pablo was the tallest Spaniard I had ever seen. Tall and lanky. He had straight black hair cut like
Paul McCartney's in his Beatles days. His apartment was sparsely furnished, like a typical student's place, with a mattress on the floor for a
bed and one chair. I sat on the chair. Pablo sat on the bed.

"So," he said, "what do you want to learn?"

"Well," I began, "I want to learn how to play my guitar in a typical
Spanish style. I mean I'm in Spain, right?" I said with a smile. "By the
way," I asked, "what part of Spain are you from?" knowing that each
region of Spain had its own style of music. I wanted him to know
that I knew that not everyone played the typical Andalusian flamenco
music.

"Actually, I'm from Argentina," Pablo said. "And I don't really
teach 'Spanish guitar,' but I can teach you some chords and some
easy songs that you can sing along with."

When he said that, I wondered if I should get up and leave. Why do I pick the one non-Spanish guitar teacher in Spain?

Remembering the long walk, I decided to give Pablo a chance and went through with the lesson. Instead of classical Spanish music, I learned how to play "Hey Jude" on my first day. Over the next two months, I also learned how to play "One" by U2, two more Beatles classics, and the fine art of fake fingerpicking. My depression didn't dissipate, but I wrote some really good songs. And then I decided Pablo lived too far to continue my lessons, and I never saw him again.

8: *La Morena*

The Black thing wasn't helping. Spanish people, I had noticed, had the peculiar habit of publicly proclaiming whatever distinguished you from the average Spaniard. That meant if you weren't a dark-haired, dark-eyed, olive-toned, small-boned conformist with a penchant for blue jeans, you would get called out. Most notably when walking down the street. An Asian walks by, you'd be likely to hear, "Toyota!" Blond girls got a *"Rubia!"* usually accompanied by a lecherous grin that implied "I'd like to get to know you better if you're interested." And I was, *"Morena!" "Negrita!" "Chocolate!"* Take your pick. Everywhere I went Spaniards shouted, whispered, and/or pointed at me, making me feel like a mutant of some sort. Fitting in was virtually impossible. And fitting in was what I thought I did best. My whole career as "the Only Black Girl in . . ." made me the Queen of Assimilation. My speech, my dress, my politics, my taste in music, everything that was me was mainstream, suburban, and easy to swallow. Except for the color of my skin, I was just like you. Get to know me and you'll realize that I am no threat. I am no different. But here in Spain, different was the first thing anybody saw, and as far as I could tell they had no interest in going any further.

But given my background, I should have been able to handle this. Adaptable was my middle name. It was my claim to fame. I could make myself comfortable at a lesbian math camp (true story) or a Sikh family reunion without breaking a sweat. My mother always likened me to a chameleon; I shifted and changed so fluidly. If I could navigate Moroccan culture, Spain shouldn't be so hard, I thought. So one day in late October, I decided that I would stop being the pitiful American and learn to blend in and become a real Spaniard for the year. I'd been scornful of the Spanish conformist mentality that dictated a strict dress code for university life: blue jeans, preferably ironed; a button-down shirt; a simple, dark-colored sweater; and the crucial adornment, a handkerchief, tied just so around the neck. Rather than bemoaning the lack of individuality, I decided to embrace the style. Sure my skin would show, but perhaps, I reasoned, the uniform would tone the black down and let me cross over into their world.

Having never been the blue-jeans type, I pulled out the closest thing I believed would do, my red jeans, and hoped they would suffice. I'd seen plenty of Spaniards in colorful jeans. Having never been the petite type, meaning I never wore tight clothing, my bulky, baggy sweaters weren't exactly screaming Spaniard, but I figured if I tucked my blue turtleneck sweater into my pants and actually wore a belt, I might get by. And for my neckerchief, I wrapped my floral-print scarf around my neck instead of my hair. I didn't know if I tied it right, but nothing was left hanging, and everything seemed neat and tucked into place. I even pulled my usually neglected hair into a neat bun at the nape of my neck. With my brand-new Spanish folder replacing the oversize green backpack I had brought from home, I thought nobody would know I was American now. I was ready to go incognegro in Spain.

Walking out of Hermi's house that day, on my way to class, I felt a new sense of optimism and excitement. "Lori," I said to myself, "you have to make your own happiness. You can't expect people to just come to you and make you their project." I agreed with myself and promised to do better. To get into Spanish life, I started making a mental list of all the things I could do to become more Spanish.

1. I'd sign up at the university for an *intercambio*, a language partner.
2. I'd stay up past 10:00 p.m. and try to go out at night and party with the locals.
3. I'd (this hurt) start talking to Kristy in Spanish and stop trying to trick her into speaking English with me.

By the time I hit the university, I was smiling from ear to ear, imagining my new life. I had to remind myself that Spaniards weren't big into toothy grins, so I quickly put on my Spanish poker face. Before heading to class I decided to stop at the *frutos secos* store for a bag of sunflower seeds to munch on. That's what the Spaniards ate for snacks. Personally I don't really care for sunflower seeds, but I was going for the fitting-in thing. Like a good Spaniard I went in and scooped my seeds out of the self-service bin and went up to the counter to pay. The owner was in a talkative mood and after weighing my seeds asked me where I was from.

"How do you know I'm not from Spain?" I answered back, teasing but kind of serious.

He laughed then. A good-natured laugh, but a laugh just the same.

"*Chica*, Spanish people don't look like you," he informed me.

"What do you mean?" I demanded. Thinking of all the people I'd seen flaunting their red jeans.

"*Eres morena*," he said, as if that explained it.

I was Black. Which meant there was no way I could be Spanish. Why had I even bothered? I untied my neckerchief then, since truth be told it was choking me. And I put my sunflower seeds back and bought a bag of potato chips instead.

Walking to class one day I watched a woman in the street try to discipline her young child. The boy was in the midst of throwing a mighty temper tantrum. I couldn't help but pause and stare as the kid was making such a fuss and his mother seemed at her wits' end, trying to keep him on his feet and still make forward progress down the street. Finally, in exasperation she threatened him with "If you don't behave, I'll give you to *that*," and she pointed directly at me. I was the *that*. I was the threat. And wouldn't you know, the boy looked into my Black face, his eyes got wide, and he immediately cut his antics short. Mom pulled him along and didn't look at me. I was shocked and angry. What was I, the boogeyman?

It didn't seem right that in 1992 Spaniards could claim ignorance for their ignorance. Sure, Spain wasn't bustling with a population of colored folks, but they watched *The Cosby Show*, *Martin*, and Steve Urkel on *Family Matters* enough to compare me to every Black female character in the thirteen to twenty-five age range. They listened to Tracy Chapman, Michael Jackson, and Stevie Wonder and watched their videos on TV. Heck, even the movie *Amistad* had been dubbed into Spanish. How could an entire country seem so unaware of, dare I say it, being politically correct? Every time I stepped into a candy shop and saw the nation's favorite chocolate candy, Conguitos, I wanted to grab the PC hotline phone and report a major crime. Conguitos, which means "little people from the Congo," are nothing more than peanut M&M's, a chocolate-covered peanut in a colorful candy shell. It's the packaging that made me want to hurt someone. The candies were sold in little plastic statues of a naked Pygmy with oversize red lips, bulging eyes, and a spear in his little hand. I just couldn't believe *I* was the only one who found naked Pygmy boy offensive. But it seemed like I was, because the only word used to describe Conguitos by Spaniards was "*deliciosos!*"

I never feared for my life because of the color of my skin. Even when I heard about the Black American student who was beaten senseless in an ice cream parlor in Madrid, I still felt safe in my little Sally (Sally was my pet name for Salamanca). I just lived in a constant state of irritation, being called out all the time. One time I thought I was going to be the victim of a hate crime. A group of about five or six boys appeared out of nowhere as soon as the door to Hermi's building slammed shut behind me. It seemed that they had been waiting for me. I rounded the corner, heading to school, and realized I was being followed. Nobody else was on the street except me and the mini–Spanish mafia. I walked faster, trying not to think about that boy in Madrid. Then they speeded up and started chanting something. Was it a call for the spillage of the Black girl's blood? I couldn't make out their words at first because the pounding in my ears of my own panic and fear was too loud. I tried to decide if I should turn around and confront them, maybe startle them with my scary black face, or perhaps I should duck onto a different street and with luck find a Good

Samaritan to save me from these children. Before I could make a decision, however, I recognized what they were saying. They were singing the jingle to the Cola Cao commercial. Cola Cao was a popular hot chocolate drink, and the box featured a bunch of African women in the sun picking cacao beans. The lyrics to the TV jingle mentioned Black women, so I guess they decided it was an appropriate taunt for *La Morena*. I found this hot chocolate ambush so hysterical, I started laughing to myself and slowed down. The boys then all ran past me in a rush, shouting at the top of their lungs *"Negrita!"* and *"Chocolate!"* and laughing all the way. This was to be a regular occurrence for the rest of the semester. It's amazing what a person can get used to.

I asked Hilary if she was having the same experiences. We hadn't struck up a real friendship, but as "sisters" in the same situation, we were automatically close. Hilary laughed at my concerns. She was enjoying herself too much to take offense at what she categorized as "just their way." Hilary seemed more street smart than I was. She didn't sweat the small stuff. She had come to Spain to practice her Spanish and have a good time and that's exactly what she was doing. She partied at night with all the other IES kids at El Skud and came to class during the daytime. The few times I had seen her at the clubs, she was always surrounded by a group of people, Spanish, American, and other. I wondered why she could deal and I couldn't. I decided Hilary and I were just two different kinds of colored girls. Whereas Hilary had come to Spain with a suitcase full of fake hair to change up her look and confuse the mess out of her host family, I decided to let my hair slowly fall out because I was unwilling to explain a no-lye relaxer to foreigners. So even though Hilary listened and clucked while I moaned about the racial slights I'd been dealing with, she didn't seem overly concerned and offered no advice beyond "you're only here for a year, just deal with it."

But I didn't know exactly how to deal with people calling me "*morena*," "hot chocolate," and sometimes marijuana (because the code name for hashish in Spanish is "chocolate." Go figure!). I didn't know how to deal with the constant stares and the pointing fingers. I didn't know how to deal with the arguments from well-meaning Spaniards telling me I couldn't call myself a real American, when I'm really from Africa! And I thought race would leave me alone this year.

Since nobody would allow me to forget my race, I became obsessed with finding others like me. I couldn't help myself, and like a thirsty man in the desert, I searched the streets of Salamanca for other Black people who could help me understand Spain's peculiar attitude toward Blackness. One time I followed a girl almost to the outer limits of the city because I thought she might be a Black Spaniard. She was wearing the black and pink jacket that just about every other Spanish student in this town wore, and she was carrying a Spanish folder with her schoolwork. She had to be a native. Her hair was unprocessed and she looked African, but she spoke Spanish like a Spaniard, with no foreign accent, as she purchased a candy bar at the kiosk where I was buying more potato chips. I didn't know what I wanted to say to her except "Are there more of us here?" But that didn't sound like a good opening so I just followed her, hoping something else would spring to my mind. But it never did and I lost her around the old bullring. On the long walk back home I realized that if some random Black person was following me around my hometown, I'd get a little freaked out, and I hoped I hadn't caused her any worry. I promised to keep my racial stalking in check. But I soon broke my promise.

"Have you met Benjamin?" Hilary asked me one day after our comparative religion class as we started walking toward the plaza.

"No, who's Benjamin?" I said.

"He's this guy who goes to Wesleyan, he's on some other program, he's one of us but you'd never know it. I met him at El Puerto de Chus last night."

"What do you mean?" I asked, wondering how Hilary managed to party every night and still be up and energetic for class in the morning. I must be so lame, considering I couldn't keep my eyes open much past 10:30 p.m.

"He's Black, right," Hilary began, "but he's so pale with this brown, shiny, curly hair, you'd never, ever guess in a million years that he's a brother."

"So how'd you find out?" I asked.

"Because this other girl who's totally in love with him told me. But that's not the freaky part. Guess who he is. You'll never guess."

"What do you mean, 'who he is'?" I said, turning to Hilary.

She stopped then for full dramatic effect.

"Benjamin, the White boy who's Black, is a great-great-great-grandson of Frederick Douglass."

"Are you serious?" I said. This was too amazing. Frederick Douglass was my hero. I had two copies of his memoir, *Narrative of the Life of Frederick Douglass, an American Slave, Written by Himself* on my bookshelf at Smith: one that was dog-eared and marked up and one that was for show. I identified with him as a Black writer and speaker who had liberated his people with his words. I wanted my words to be that powerful someday.

Then I stopped. "How do you know for sure that he's really his great-great-great-grandson? Did he tell you that?"

"Hell yeah," Hilary said, laughing. "I asked him straight up. He seemed kind of embarrassed, but he confirmed it."

"What was he like?" I pushed. "What else did he say?"

Hilary put her hand up like a crossing guard stopping traffic.

"Whoa there, lady. I didn't ask him for a full autobiography. We were in a club full of people, remember? But he seemed nice and I'm sure we'll hang out sometime."

Short of sounding like a Negro-intellectual groupie, I stopped myself from asking Hilary to invite me along whenever she planned on hanging with Benjamin. Instead I just asked her to point him out the next time she saw him and I was around.

Once she did, Benjamin became my new obsession.

I don't know why I was so obsessed, but I chased Benjamin around like I was Indiana Jones looking for the Holy Grail. Like this Benjamin might hold some sacred truth about Blackness. Like he might channel the spirit of his famous ancestor to teach me something about myself. Oh, and he was also really cute. Hilary didn't mention that part. He had a milky white complexion dotted with deep red freckles

across his nose, curly hair and perfect white teeth in a round che-
rubic face. But in a hot boy kind of way. Maybe he wasn't that hot,
but I mixed my historical obsession with romantic crush and voilà, I
became a stalker. Again. Hilary did get a chance to introduce us one
night when I forced myself to stay out late and party. So on occasion
when we passed on the streets or in a club or bar, I nodded my head
in his general direction and tried not to let my fanaticism show. I even
knew where he lived and spent significant amounts of time hovering
around his doorway waiting for him to emerge. I now wonder if I had
put in as much time studying the economies of southern Europe as I
put in studying Benjamin, I could have earned more than a B– in my
economics class.

Finally I had enough. I hadn't told anybody about my obsession,
because I didn't think anybody would understand. I mentioned Benjamin's existence in Salamanca to Brook to gauge her response. Since
she didn't jump up and down and squeal with excitement, I kept my almost criminal behavior close to the vest. But something had to change.
I felt like a junkie who'd been staying high on multiple mini-doses
of crack. I was tired of the contact high and wanted to go all the way
or stop already with the fantasies. So one day after hovering around
Benjamin's building for close to an hour, alternating between sweating and going cold with anxiety, I rang the button to his apartment. I
prayed desperately that he was home, yet hoped with all my heart that
he wasn't so I could spare myself the embarrassment that was sure to
follow. But then I remembered that this was how it was done in Spain.
Visiting friends. Nobody had phones in their apartments to arrange
dates and get-togethers. If you wanted to talk to someone you just
showed up at their doorstep. It was a very un-American custom—to
drop in uninvited—but we weren't in America.

"Yes?" I recognized his voice through the intercom.

"Um, hi, Benjamin, it's Lori—can I come up?"

"Sure," he said and buzzed me up. What a relief he didn't say "Lori
who?" or "What do you want?" This was a good sign.

As I walked up the stairs to his second-floor apartment, I prepped
my speech. I was just going to be honest and tell him about my ob-

session and ask him about his family. That's really all I wanted to know . . . and if he fell in love with me in the process, then so be it. I had decided that having a crush on a white-looking boy, but one who was Black with a historical pedigree, would be acceptable to the race police. My loyalty to the cause could not be questioned on the arm of Frederick Douglass's seed.

Benjamin opened the door and gave me his perfect smile. I felt my knees buckle but tried not to show it. I tried to act casual and confident. Like it was perfectly normal and harmless that I was in his home even though we barely knew each other. My eyes roamed around the room looking for clues that would link this boy to Frederick Douglass. I didn't see anything that caught my eye, but I also didn't know what I was looking for, either. Pictures? A copy of one his famous speeches? A lock of that famous hair?

"You want to see the apartment?" Benjamin asked.

"Sure," I said. "A couple of friends and I are looking for an apartment for next semester. How'd you get such a great place?"

"Oh, I got lucky," he said. "A friend from Brown had it last year and gave me the number of the owner, so I arranged it all before I even got here."

It was a really big three-bedroom apartment in a nice section of Sally. He was lucky.

"So the reason I stopped by," I started as we sat on a futon in the salon, "is that I'm kind of obsessed with you." How's that for an opening line? No pressure at all.

Benjamin looked weirded out, so I rushed to finish my thought. Honesty, honesty, I chanted to myself.

"I mean with your great-great-great-grandfather. Are you really related to Frederick Douglass?"

"Yeah," he said.

"Wow, that's so cool. I mean, you're like living history," I said.

"I guess so." Benjamin shrugged. "I don't really think about it that much."

My fantasies began to deflate. I tried another tactic. "Do you have any pictures or anything that belonged to him?"

"Someone in my family does," he said. And then nothing.

Okay, this conversation was not going anywhere. Where was the deep, meaningful conversation about Black history and Frederick's legacy and the true meaning of race? I thought if I just brought it up, Benjamin would take the ball and run, leading us into an almost spiritual level of intellectual contemplation of our place in this world.

"So do you feel like any connection to him whatsoever?" I said, desperate now for Benjamin the real person to measure up to Benjamin my fantasy Negro emancipator.

"Not really," he said and flashed me another smile. Could it be possible that the great-great-great-grandson of one of the most important Black men of the nineteenth century was just kind of apolitical and without a racial agenda? I couldn't bear the thought.

I had nothing else to say and no reason to pretend.

"Okey-dokey, then," I said. "I'm done. Thanks for answering all of my little questions."

"Yeah, sure," he said as he walked me to the door.

By the time I'd walked out of his building my disappointment had been replaced with a palpable sense of relief that my Benjamin obsession was over.

9: If You Want My Body, and You Think I'm Sexy . . .

There was another side to the story. Being Black in Spain meant I was different, but it also meant that I was sexy, something I'd never been before. I knew I wasn't ugly. I knew my features were on the cute side of normal. If I put some effort into it, I could actually be attractive, bordering on pretty. But usually I didn't bother to make the effort. In a way it was self-preservation. The White boys in my world—at school, in my neighborhood, on the swim team—didn't seem to be interested in me, so if I acted uninterested in their affections, I felt in control.

I assumed boys didn't ask me out in high school because of the race thing. Even though I had countless crushes and could flirt with the best of them, I had no idea if any of them ever truly desired me. Back in the first grade, I had this special friend, Andy Taylor. Andy and I played all the time. It helped that his sister and my sister were also friends and our mothers got along well. One day at recess, Andy, Claire Evans, and I were playing on the jungle gym when we decided to ask Andy whom he liked better. I just knew he'd pick me, but he took his time answering and seemed to be thinking deeply. Finally he announced that he had to choose Claire because she was White and so was he. It was a first-grade lesson I never forgot.

After that, I basically kept my desires and secret crushes on White boys to myself. Never again did I want to be rejected because I'm Black. Unfortunately, that put my options for romance at close to zero growing up. But I didn't mind. I satisfied my desires with copious amounts of Harlequin Romance novels, followed by an almost fanatic devouring of thick bodice-ripper historical romances. And I adopted the role of listener and advice giver (based on theory, of course) to all my friends. After a while, I just kind of assumed that I probably lacked what others might call sex appeal. I mean if I really had it, wouldn't somebody besides some desperate Moroccan men and a really sweet Spanish exchange student have told me by now? Even my flings at college had evolved from meetings of the mind, not the body. The boys had been intellectual and quirky types and I gathered they liked me for my bubbly personality and quick wit and not my rockin' bod.

In Spain, my theory about myself was challenged to the extreme. I had more male attention in one semester than I'd had in my whole life. When I went out at night, invariably a Spanish guy would whisper *morena* in my ear with such longing and ask me to dance, or watch me dance with an unwavering gaze. Bartenders, police officers, and the eighteen-year-old boy I was tutoring in English in exchange for motorcycle-riding lessons all propositioned me.

At first the attention felt spectacular. Like finally somebody was appreciating my brown skin, womanly curves, and juicy lips. I no longer had to pretend that I didn't enjoy male attention. I grew heady with this knowledge and started to play the part, wearing tight black pants without a long, ass-covering top. None of my clothes qualified as ho-gear, but I began wearing them in different ways that didn't begin and end with covering my assets. At the dance clubs, I accepted offers to dance with different guys and would actually sandwich a guy between myself and a friend, shaking my rump and gyrating like a stripper on a pole.

So when this guy named Antonio approached me one night at Puerto de Chus, having watched my antics on the dance floor all night, I let him buy me a drink. And when he gave me his address and made me promise to come over the following day, I said I would. And I did. Antonio was a law student. He was tall with black, shiny hair. He was so not my type. He had chest hair, which poked out at the top of the polo shirts he liked to wear. I have a thing about chest hair. It usually disqualifies a guy instantly, but I was drawn to Antonio's überconfident style and decided to overlook the chest rug. When I got to his apartment, I experienced a moment of panic. How did I know Antonio, if that was his real name, wasn't a serial killer with a taste for dark meat? What if I was walking into some horrible trap? What if he lured girls into his apartment and raped and tortured them? With these vivid images in my mind, I rang his doorbell instead of running away as fast as possible.

Instead of a serial killer, I found Antonio in shorts and a T-shirt and a pair of brown bedroom slippers that looked like the kind my eighty-year-old grandfather in Baltimore liked to wear. He kissed me on both cheeks and I decided I had no reason to be afraid. After sitting with Antonio in his living room watching a soccer match on TV with very limited conversation between us, I also realized I had no reason to be there at all.

"So, I'm going to go now," I announced after sitting through an entire hour of *fútbol*.

"Already?" he whined. "You just got here."

"Yeah, but Antonio, we're not doing anything. This is not how you treat a woman when you invite her to your apartment for the first time," I said, emboldened by the fact that I knew this man desired me. I pointed to the dirty clothes and clutter lying about. "And you should have cleaned up, too. Why would I want to stay here?"

I had never spoken to anyone like that before, especially a guy. An older guy at that. But I couldn't help myself. It's how I felt and I had nothing to lose. That had kind of become my mantra during my year abroad: "You have nothing to lose, so go ahead and do the things you've always been afraid of and never had a chance to experience." I considered this year in Spain my parenthesis from reality.

"Please stay," Antonio pleaded.

"Nope. I'm leaving." I wasn't trying to torture the poor guy. I just didn't want to be there anymore.

"Well, will you let me make it up to you?" he asked.

"How?" I asked.

"Come over on Friday and I'll cook dinner for you."

Now he was talking. Besides the fact that he'd be providing me with an excuse for not eating one of Hermi's well-intentioned but invariably lousy meals, I loved the idea of a man who knew his way around a kitchen.

"Bueno," I said nonchalantly. "But I'm still leaving now. I don't like *fútbol.*"

Antonio kissed me good-bye on both cheeks and I promised to return.

Had I been in the realm of my real life, after the chest hair, after the *fútbol* date, I would have pulled out my own eyelashes before returning to Antonio's house. But I was making bad decisions out of loneliness and throwing caution to the wind thanks to my newfound sex appeal, which made me bold and stupid. And to be perfectly honest, the other factor at play was that I just liked the attention.

On Friday, I went back to Antonio's, hoping he'd taken my suggestions and made some effort at entertaining me. I wanted to be wooed. I wanted some romance to bring some sparkle into my life in Salamanca. Having failed at blending into the Spanish landscape legitimately, I now planned on sneaking in the back way, by attaching myself to a man. Before I left the States all of my friends teased me about the Latin lover I was sure to find, but I had dismissed such suggestions as beneath me and my mission to conquer Spain. "I am not going to fall in love," I swore. "Why would I go and do that only to have to break up at the end of the year? Who needs that kind of drama?" And then, just to prove my point, "Besides, it's such a tacky cliché to have your little junior-year-abroad romance." That wasn't going to happen to me, I vowed then. But now things had changed and I opened the door to the possibility of acquiring a special friend, *if* it would help me have a more authentic experience.

Based on the smells emanating from Antonio's kitchen when I returned, there was no reason to believe this relationship had a future.

This time his apartment was tidier and he had managed to wear real clothes, although the granddaddy bedroom slippers still adorned his feet. After kissing cheek to cheek to say hello, Antonio ushered me into the kitchen where the tiny table was set. I guess I didn't warrant setting the dining room table. I decided this was more intimate and romantic.

"Sit," Antonio told me. So I sat. And he turned to the stove, removing pot tops and making a bit of noise. He then served me a plate with two very greasy fried hot dogs, a greasy fried egg that was still raw and runny around the yolk, and a slice of white bread. Before I could stop myself, I opened my mouth and said, " This is dinner?" Even Hermi did better than this. "I thought you said you wanted to cook for me," I said, trying to mask my disappointment as I tried to inconspicuously wipe off some of the oil that was now congealing on my hot dog.

"Well, I don't know how to cook," Antonio admitted.

"Then why did you invite me for dinner?" I almost shouted with exasperation.

"Because I wanted to show you that I could make you dinner. I am not a *machista*," he added.

For some reason, Antonio had it in his head that I, like every other American woman, believed all Spanish men hadn't evolved past the Neanderthals when it came to feminism and equality between the sexes. He liked to remind me constantly that he wanted to get to know me for my mind and that if we were to get married (what!) he'd definitely help around the house. Like cooking dinner.

I really wanted to like Antonio. He seemed to be trying so hard. And his English was good enough so we could have conversations about abstract ideas like feminism and Spanish law and the difference between American and Spanish culture. So I settled down and tried to ignore the pool of grease that my food was swimming in. I kept my eyes focused on Antonio's eyes and didn't let them wander down to his tuft of chest hair that seemed to be taunting me. And I stopped berating myself for being so weak of spirit that I was forcing myself to talk to a guy who was sooo not my type because it beat sitting at home composing more sad songs to sing with the guitar.

"What? What are you staring at?" I asked Antonio. The conversation had come to an abrupt halt, basically because Antonio was no longer listening to me. He was off on another plane.

His eyes came back into focus.

We were now in the salon, having finished dinner, and still enjoying our conversation. I was feeling a lot more comfortable and in the back of my mind upgrading Antonio from mistake to perhaps first real Spanish friend. The conversation had been flowing, until now.

"I'm staring at your lips," Antonio announced.

I felt a shiver of despair race down my spine.

"Why?" I asked, even though I knew I shouldn't.

"Because I want to kiss them," he answered, looking at me expectantly.

"Well, you can't," I said.

"Why not?" he asked, looking truly perplexed.

"Because I just met you and I don't kiss people I just met," I explained.

And then his law school training kicked in. "Well, technically you've known me for over a month, because we met at Puerto de Chus four weeks ago. How long do you need to know someone before you kiss him?"

I didn't have an answer because I hadn't kissed enough people to have a rule. But Antonio didn't need to know that.

"Like three months," I hedged.

"Three months," he repeated, like I had just given him three months to live. "*Joder, mujer, estás loca.*" And with that, he just leaned over, practically pinning me underneath his burly frame, and kissed me. Apparently the thought of waiting for three more months didn't sit too well with Antonio.

I tried to relax. I tried to enjoy it. I tried to imagine myself anywhere but there. And that's when I realized that if I had to work so hard to enjoy a kiss, then I needed to put a stop to it. At first Antonio thought my squirming and pushing meant I was being turned on, and he let out a happy little groan. He continued to swish his what seemed to be abnormally small tongue around my mouth while depositing what seemed to be excessive amounts of saliva down my throat. I knew if I didn't put a stop to this attack, I'd be revisiting my greasy dinner.

So with two hands I gave Antonio a mighty shove and he sat up.

Looking at his wet lips still parted with anticipation and the gleam in his eye, I just turned around and ran out of his apartment, yelling "Good-bye" and "See you later" to his astonished face. I didn't stop running until I was halfway home. There was a bakery ahead and I ran right inside and bought the biggest piece of cake on display and shoved the whole thing in my mouth, trying to rid myself of the memory and taste of Antonio.

...

I avoided El Puerto de Chus after that. And took pains never to walk by Antonio's apartment, going blocks out of my way if necessary to avoid accidentally running into him. Just saying the name "Antonio" made me feel nauseous. Because of the kiss, the food, and my own weakness for hanging out with a guy I had no interest in. I had spent twenty years without regular male companionship; I didn't need to get a man now. Antonio had taught me that my fantasies were far more palatable than being with just a random warm body, even if he did have a sexy accent. I decided to stay true to my real self and leave the boys alone.

But they wouldn't leave me alone. As sloppily as I often dressed, as neglected as I left my hair, Spanish men still found me desirable.

"Excuse me, are you Naomi Campbell?" a man asked me in a dance club one night.

"*Guapa,*" the little old men whose job it was to sit in the Plaza Mayor and comment on life would shout at me when I walked by.

And it felt good to be desired. I felt powerful. My self-confidence, always at high levels, climbed a little bit higher. But then I read an article in the Sunday paper. I noticed it in the magazine section because of the pictures. There were beautiful black models interspersed with African prints and wild animals, and the headline read "*Salvaje.*" The gist of the story was that Black women were so beautiful (good) because there was something about us that was still wild (bad). In essence the article explained the Black woman's hypersexuality through our intrinsically savage nature. I threw the paper down in disgust and hoped nobody else read it and wanted to discuss it with me. Or worse, comment on my intrinsically hypersexed nature.

But then it all made sense. All this attention I was getting wasn't about men wanting to be my one true love. They wanted to be my one true lover, getting buck wild with the Black beast. It was just another stereotype the Spanish had about Blackness that was hard to refute since there didn't seem to be any Black people around to change their minds. My language partner, Carlos, sat down one day and told me a joke in English. The punch line had to do with the infinite size of a Black woman's vagina, and he couldn't stop laughing when he told

me. I was angered and sickened and embarrassed. He didn't understand why I was upset.

"Don't you get why that joke might be offensive to me?" I asked him.

"It's a joke. It was funny," he said, still smiling.

"Do you think I want to hear a joke about my own genitalia?" I
asked, willing him to understand my point.

"The joke wasn't about you," he said solemnly, as if that would
clear things up.

"But I'm a Black woman," I said through clenched teeth. I hated
this conversation. I hated having to defend and explain and educate
the Spanish about Negritude and about cultural sensitivity. I was tired
of being the teacher.

I couldn't wait for the Christmas holidays. I was going to Belgium
for two weeks to stay with my sister, who was working for NATO. I
needed out of España. Even though Belgium wasn't home, I needed
to get reacquainted with the old me. This new me was freaking me
out with her out-there sexiness. I decided to swear off men for the
rest of my trip and focus on me. Even though I had never done so before, I decided I needed to purify myself through a ceremony of some
sort. So I waited until Kristy went out on one of her many dates (poor
Wayne had been quickly forgotten) and got myself completely naked.
I put on my robe and lit a candle. I then pulled out a lock of my hair
and clipped a fingernail. Then I took a flower petal from the bouquet
in our room and added that to my body parts and burned them all. I
then stood out on the balcony and scattered the ashes of the old, bad,
sinful me and prayed to the moon that I be reborn. I prayed really,
really hard to be returned to my regular self, proud and independent
and focused. I promised myself I would not under any circumstances
get involved with the male species. I came back inside and blew out
the candle, put my pajamas on, and climbed into bed. Second semester was going to be much better. Brook and I had decided to get an
apartment together with a German friend of Brook's. I was starting
to make friends with two of the girls from my program, and my head
had finally stopped hurting from thinking all day in Spanish. Boys
had been a time-consuming distraction and I was officially done.

⚜ 1 0: Rupert

Coming back to Salamanca after Christmas felt like coming home. Our new apartment on Calle Sancti Spiritus was a furnished two-bedroom with a tiny kitchen, a salon, and one bathroom. We didn't have an oven, but there was a washing machine in the kitchen. Brook and I got busy right away turning the generic-looking apartment into a comfortable nest. The first thing we had to do was find two more roommates because our German friend had been called back home to Deutschland after her parents surmised she was wasting her time and their money in España. We quickly found another American, Claudia, who wanted out of her *señora*'s home because the woman couldn't or wouldn't comprehend that vegetarian meant that Claudia would never, ever, eat meat, not even just a little bit for flavor. The three of us all agreed that our fourth roommate had to be Spanish or this little experiment in international living would be a bust. So we posted flyers around the university and soon enough María came into our lives.

María was from Valladolid. Even though she had the most common Spanish name, there was nothing ordinary about her. For starters, she was half Russian. Her second surname was an unpronounceable jumble of consonants. Her mother was Russian but had married a Spaniard and moved to Spain. María spoke no Russian, but every Spaniard who met her for the first time said she spoke with an accent of some sort. Well, that accent was due to the fact that she spent much of her childhood in South America. María was twenty-four and busy working on her master's degree in education. She adored cigarettes, black coffee, and foreign boys with blond hair and green eyes. And while she was waiting for her blond prince to whisk her off into the sunset, when we first met her, she was romantically involved with her middle-aged archery coach. Never one to sit idly by, María managed to squeeze in a semiprofessional archery career in her spare time. She was full of surprises and we loved her for it. And she loved us. All of us. María was our portal into Spanish culture, although with María it was slightly off to the left of center. But she took her job seriously as the messiah of all things Spanish to us, her youthful disciples.

Still pure from my moonlit ceremony, I promised myself that this second and final semester in Spain would be taken seriously. I was going to do well in my classes, find some extracurricular activity to occupy my time, and become totally fluent. Or else. Living with Brook was a big help. She was an eternal optimist and a fountain of ideas that required lots of time and little money. Like preparing an entire Indian meal without spending more than the five dollars we had between us to buy ingredients. Or figuring out how to make chocolate chip cookies without an oven.

By February, when my twenty-first birthday rolled around, I felt at peace in my new Spanish home and happy with my life. I threw myself a birthday party to celebrate my new year and the new me. The new me was calm and reflective and able to deal with her role as Black ambassador to Spain. I accepted the fact that I would always be *la morena* and let those irritating comments from strangers slide off my back. I felt like the old Lori, in control of her world again. I even managed to finagle an internship at a local elementary school complete with a teacher mentor who liked to debate and discuss education theory with me over coffee in the Plaza Mayor. I recognized me again.

So when I started noticing Cute Boy in my German class again, I felt okay with my crush. It wasn't desperation making me notice his beautiful smile and his delicate hands or his perfect nose. I just wanted to talk to him. Find out why he was always late to class, why he usually arrived surrounded by a posse of women. Where did he get that Rutgers University sweatshirt? And besides, having something to focus on in German class, besides what Max and Melanie were buying at the market, helped me keep my eyes open instead of nodding off from utter boredom.

"Do you even know his name?" Olivia was asking me, trying to keep the frustration out of her voice but not doing a very good job as we sat in a café by the plaza. Olivia actually wasn't American. She was Belgian but went to college in Ohio, already spoke four languages, and was in Spain perfecting her almost fluent Spanish. You could almost hate her if you were that type. I didn't hate her at all because besides the fact that she was quite nice with a droll sense of humor, she had been to the States over the Christmas break and brought back bagels! I'd have been a fool to hate Olivia.

"Yes, his name is Manuel," I said. I had managed to speak to Cute Boy on a couple of occasions, but I was always tongue-tied and nervous. I didn't want him to think I was trying to flirt or that I was throwing myself at him. It appeared he already had enough female attention. I had to be extra careful because I had two strikes against me. I was an American and Black, which to a Spanish man translates to "easy whore."

"So you've spoken with him," Claudia chimed in, sounding hopeful.

"Well, kind of," I stammered. Olivia and Claudia were staying in Salamanca for the whole year, but we had only recently started hanging out. I liked them both. They were serious students and pretty much only hung out together and with other international students. A gathering at their cozy attic apartment in the heart of the Plaza Mayor meant Spanish, French, and English would be spoken, and fantastic food, thanks to Claudia, would always be available.

"What does 'kind of' mean?" Olivia asked, raising a doubtful eyebrow.

"Well, I asked him if I could borrow his pencil one time. And another time I asked him what page we were on." Even to my own ears I sounded like I was twelve instead of twenty-one. In the States I was the most outgoing, gregarious person. In a foreign language I'd become a social retard.

"Well, I'm tired of hearing you going on and on about this boy and not doing something about it," Olivia said.

"I'm trying to," I whined. "I'm just working at my own pace."

"Well, at this rate," Olivia said, "you're going to have to be pen pals, because we're going home in four months."

"I don't know what to say to him," I confessed. And it was true. In my mind I had tried out several different conversation openers and they all sounded lame and disingenuous. And I still wasn't sure how to strike up a conversation in Spanish. Really, these were the kinds of linguistic nuances I wish they taught you in Advanced Conversation: How to flirt without coming off like a whore.

"Just talk," Olivia said, like it was the easiest thing in the world.

"About what?" I asked.

"About anything. I mean, how hard is it?" she asked.

"It's hard," I responded, not wanting to mention my fear of being rejected or mistaken for a slut.

"You know what?" Olivia said with a steely resolve in her voice. "I'm coming to class with you. I want to see why this boy has gotten you all tied up. I mean, let's see if he's even worth it."

"You can't just come to my German class," I protested.

"Why not? I speak German," she said. "And there are so many people in the class, the professor probably won't even notice. Don't worry about it."

"Okay," I said, already worrying that somehow I was going to regret this decision. But it was true, there were at least fifty students in the class and the professor hardly ever looked up from his lectern.

"When's your next class?" Olivia demanded.

"Friday," I said, still wondering if I should stop this thing.

"Okay, I'll meet you in front of Anaya on Friday at nine o'clock," she said.

And that was that.

Olivia made it look so easy. As soon as we got to the classroom, she made me point Manuel out. And then we sat right behind him. She made me introduce her as if Manuel and I were buddies. But he seemed really happy to meet her. And he smiled at me. Throughout class she'd whisper things to him and he'd whisper back, and for a moment I panicked and worried that he was going to fall in love with her instead of me. But then I remembered that I wasn't interested in romance, just friendship, and if he was a friend of Olivia's, then we could all be friends. So I just sat back and watched Olivia do in forty-five minutes what I hadn't been able to accomplish in six weeks.

After class, Manuel, Olivia, and I lingered and walked slowly together from the university to the Plaza Mayor, talking and laughing
and getting to know one another. Now I knew that Manuel came from
the south of Spain and he lived in a dorm near the bus station and
across the street from the cemetery. No wonder I had never bumped
into him outside of school. He lived in no-man's-land. He told us it
usually took him thirty minutes to walk to school each day. That could
explain why he was always late to class. When we reached the plaza,
Manuel said good-bye and the three of us went our separate ways.

On Monday, I wondered if Manuel would speak to me again or,
without Olivia to run interference, if I would be back to asking him
simple sentences about German grammar. He arrived late as usual but
sat close to me in the back of the room. After class he asked if I was
walking home and we repeated our slow stroll to the plaza, making
small talk all the way. I found out that his full name was Manuel Jesús
Malia Camacho. And that he was a huge basketball fan and followed the
NBA like a fanatic. When I told him I was from Milwaukee, instead of
mentioning serial killer Jeffrey Dahmer like most Spaniards, he told me
the name of the arena where the Milwaukee Bucks played and what the
maximum seating capacity was. I found that endearing. He asked me
if I was a vegetarian like so many of these other Americans, and I said
no, but explained my current circumstances. Namely, that because I depended on the generosity of my parents for spending money, I had very
little funds to buy food, especially meat. So I had become very adept,
with Brook's help, at making lentils, garbanzo beans, and eggs taste like
meat. I had always been a happy carnivore, but my frugal, meat-free diet
didn't bother me. But it bothered Manuel. He worried that a meal without meat must feel like deprivation. It was a constant concern of his as
our casual acquaintanceship grew into a casual friendship, sustained
wholly on our walks from class to the plaza.

We started walking slower to have more time to talk, and Manuel
stopped allowing his other female friends to stroll with us so we could
just talk to each other. I sensed their resentment, but I didn't care.
Manuel had so many questions about the States and about the English
language. He was studying philology and loved to dissect languages

until he knew the origin and meaning of every word. He often came to me with questions about the subtle difference between two words in English that I had never heard of and I'd have to disappoint him with my ignorance. When we weren't playing word games, Manuel regaled me with stories of the south of Spain, painting a picture of a paradise I told him I'd like to visit sometime.

Finally one day in late March, the conversation turned once again to the meat-free lifestyle. By this time it was kind of a joke between us.

"I just don't think I could ever feel satisfied with a meal if there wasn't any meat involved," Manuel said as we came to the end of our walk. To the place where he turned left and I turned right.

And before I thought it through, I responded, "I bet I could make you an entire vegetarian dinner and you'd be totally satisfied."

Without missing a beat, he said, "Okay, when?"

I tried not to act flustered, realizing that we were about to take this safe walking-home-together friendship into the realm of my home. Breathe deep, Lori, I told myself. I calculated in my head. Today was Wednesday; I needed a full day to gather ingredients and a full day to cook. "Well, um, how about Friday?"

"Okay," Manuel said, seeming way too casual. "What time?"

"Nine o'clock." I said, resorting to the official dinner hour in Spain.

"Great, I'll see you on Friday," he said. And then he turned left, and I went right.

Friday morning I woke up in a panic. The dough for the *croquetas* was chilling in the refrigerator, the lentils were soaking, and the refrigerator was stocked with all the ingredients I needed for the soup. But still I felt like I was forgetting something. I dragged myself into the kitchen to find Brook and Claudia smiling at me.

"Tonight's the big night. Are you excited?" Claudia teased. My roommates were very much aware of my infatuation with Manuel.

I groaned. "Why in the world did I agree to do this?"

"Do you want me to help you make anything?" Brook asked.

"No," I said. "I have to make everything myself. It's part of the deal."

"Are you sure you want us to be here?" Claudia asked. "We could very easily disappear for the evening."

"Oh my God, no," I said. "You guys are my buffer. I mean if things go really bad and he turns out to be a total jerk or something, I don't have to deal with him by myself." I wanted this to be a dinner party, not a date. Less pressure. I experienced a momentary Antonio flashback and feared a repeat performance. Manuel seemed decent, but who knew if he was just waiting to pounce as soon as my guard went down.

María, who spoke no English, came into the kitchen for her morning cup of coffee. She asked us what we were talking about. Brook, who spoke Spanish better than Claudia and I, quickly caught her up on my growing anxiety.

"*Hija*," María started, "don't ever get this worked up over a boy. Just cook the food and enjoy yourself. He'll be just one more at the table."

María was so practical. I loved her no-nonsense approach to life.

So I got dressed and started to cook. The meal would begin with crispy potato *croquetas*, followed by a hearty lentil stew, rice, and bread. Dessert would be my famous alternative to baked apples, *manzanas a la microonda*, apples in the microwave.

By 2:00 p.m. the *croquetas* were rolled and dipped in bread crumbs ready for me to fry and the lentils were still soaking, so I took a nap. When I woke up I decided we needed a green salad, so I raced to the market and bought lettuce, which in Spain constitutes a salad.

By 6:00 p.m. I had achieved a level of calmness that allowed me to function normally. But then the doorbell rang. I checked the clock. There was no way Manuel was three hours early. Thankfully, it wasn't him. It was Mike, the Canadian drifter Brook had befriended. He showed up periodically to bemoan his lack of purpose in life, to get a free meal, or to teach me how to play a new chord on my guitar. Tonight he was angling for the free meal.

"I'm having a guest over for dinner," I said to Mike as he made himself comfortable at the kitchen table.

"Oh, don't mind me," he said. "I'll be out of your way soon. I just needed to experience some human kindness and your place is always filled with it." He then just sighed and looked pathetic.

"What's the matter, Mike?" I asked, stirring my enormous pot of lentils. I knew I was making way too much food, but I kind of over-compensated for the lack of meat by making insane quantities of everything. I'd promised Manuel he'd leave satisfied.

"Nothing," Mike said and sighed again.

"Come on, Mike," I coaxed, "out with it."

And so it began, Mike's never-ending sob story of trying to make this one particular Spanish woman fall in love with him. He barely spoke any Spanish and didn't have much to offer, considering he lived only one step above a hobo. But he was so earnest and so wounded, it was hard to do what we should have done and kicked him in the pants and told him to snap out of it. Instead I offered my only form of comfort.

"Do you want to stay for dinner, Mike?" I asked, hoping he'd say no.

"Well, since it looks like you're making enough to feed a small army, I guess I'll stay," he said as he began to unwrap his scarf and shrug off his top layer of clothing.

"*Hola*, Mike," María said, smiling as she came into the kitchen. María found Mike entirely amusing. He was such the anti–Spanish male. There was nothing macho about him. Plus, since he couldn't speak Spanish very well, his clumsy attempts to communicate with María made him that much more comical.

María turned to me. "My dinner plans fell through, so I'll be here for dinner, too. I can't wait," she said with a gleam in her eyes.

So adding María and Mike to the dinner party brought the number up to six. Six people crowded around our little kitchen table built for two. I'd have to pull out the ironing board for overflow items. Then I realized that since Mike didn't speak Spanish and María didn't speak English, this was going to be a very interesting evening.

At 9:00 p.m. everything was ready. The table was set and I had changed into my "I changed but I'm not dressed up" outfit. It was a navy blue Esprit baby doll dress with large white buttons. I thought I looked cute but casual. At 9:05, Manuel hadn't shown up and I began to worry. Maybe he forgot. We didn't have a telephone, so if something happened, he couldn't call to cancel. At 9:15 María declared him an official no-show, adding that she wasn't surprised because all men are genetically predisposed to disappoint us. We didn't bother to translate that for Mike. I went into the bathroom to cry. All that effort and energy wasted. But before I dissolved into tears, I remembered my no-man, no-cry vow and reminded myself what was really important in life. I had a kitchen full of friends ready to enjoy my dinner and if this guy didn't show, no big deal. More food for us.

I came out of the bathroom and announced that dinner would be served in five minutes. And that's when the doorbell rang. Of course, it was Manuel.

I opened the door to his fresh-scrubbed, smiling face.

"You're late," I said as a greeting.

"No, I'm not," he said, sweeping past me and entering the apartment.

"We said nine o'clock," I said. "And it's now nine twenty."

"I know," he said, still smiling and obviously not noticing my agitation.

"Well, it's nine twenty," I repeated, trying not to notice my heart doing backflips of happiness that he had showed up.

He stopped and turned to look me straight in the face to explain. "I'm from the south, so technically I had until ten o'clock before I'd really be considered late."

I had to laugh. That was the first thing we had been taught at orientation here in Spain. The concept of time was a very fluid thing. Deadlines were guidelines. And it was true, if you said you were going to meet someone for drinks at six, not until seven o'clock rolled around could you get even slightly worried that they might be late.

So I forgave this smiling Spaniard in front of me and ushered him into the kitchen where eight eyes were ready to size him up.

I made the introductions and told Manuel to sit down at the one remaining chair at the table. I didn't plan on eating because I was too nervous and I had to serve. I turned to the food then and an awkward silence hung in the air. Brook started to speak to Manuel in Spanish, and María quickly joined in the conversation. But Manuel noticed Mike and Claudia's blank stares, and I quickly summed it up. "María doesn't speak English, Mike doesn't really speak Spanish, and Claudia is somewhere in between."

"Okay," Manuel said, and then he sealed his place in my heart forever because for the next forty-five minutes of my dinner, he played international diplomat, keeping the conversation light and flowing, speaking in English then translating quickly to Spanish for María. I could tell she approved because she turned off her skeptical face and turned on the flirtatious face that she usually reserved for tall, blond foreigners with green eyes.

By the time the last sticky sweet *manzana* had been devoured, sweat was rolling down my back and there was still half a pot of lentils left, despite the fact that Manuel had polished off three full bowls. I sampled the stew and was disappointed that it lacked the rich, hearty flavor of my previous attempts at that typical Spanish dish. But Manuel complimented me on everything and announced at the end of the meal that he was indeed satisfied, but that a pork chop would have gone well as a second course. I had to laugh, because I secretly agreed.

Brook and Amy jumped up and demanded that I remove myself from the kitchen; they took over cleanup. María dashed off to meet up with some other friends, and Mike headed out into the night to earn some coins with his guitar playing. Manuel and I went into the salon, which also happened to double as my bedroom (a recurring theme in my life abroad). I collapsed onto the couch, exhausted from all my preparations. Manuel walked around the room, looking at the pictures and postcards I had posted on the wall to remind me of home. We made small talk, both of us unsure where this next phase of the "date" was supposed to go. Before we fell into silence I grabbed my homework folder and pulled out an assignment from my class on gender in Mediterranean societies.

"Do you want to help me with my homework?" I asked Manuel.

He came to sit next to me on the couch.

"Sure," he said. "What do you need?"

"Well, I have this survey I have to ask at least ten people to complete. And they have to be Spanish because we're studying the role of the woman in Spanish society," I explained.

Manuel looked a little skeptical, like this didn't sound like a fun way to end a date, so I quickly assured him that the questions were easy and pretty interesting.

Secretly I wanted him to answer so I could gauge just how *machista* he was. I figured all Spanish men carried the *machista* gene, so it was crucial to find out how deeply embedded into his personality it really was. I reasoned that based on how he answered these questions, I'd be able to tell if he was really someone I'd want to be friends with. Or if I should cut him off now.

There were twenty questions on the survey. It usually took fifteen minutes when I had done it with other people. Two and half hours later, Manuel and I were still on question number seven. I didn't think it possible, but I had found a boy who liked to talk as much as I did. At 1:00 a.m. Manuel noticed the hour and looked at me with a stricken expression.

"I'm so sorry, I didn't realize the time. I should leave, it's probably too late for me to be here."

I responded calmly. "Manuel, I'm really enjoying our conversation. When it gets to be too late for you to be here, I'll let you know." And with that, he relaxed back into his seat and we continued to discuss how a family could function best with two parents working. Manuel's mother had gone back to work even though she didn't have to when Manuel was around eleven. My mother had always worked, but managed to make us think we were her full-time job since she snuck off to her third-shift nursing job while we slept. Later when my sister and I were old enough, my mom went back to school and got her master's degree and began a very successful career as a psychotherapist.

At four o'clock in the morning, with my eyelids taking more and more time to recover after each blink, I put a halt to the conversation and informed Manuel that now it *was* late and he had to leave. I couldn't hold my yawns in anymore and I didn't want Manuel to think he was boring me. Because he wasn't. He started to apologize again for staying so late, and I had to assure him that just because I was kicking him out now didn't mean I didn't enjoy every moment of our conversation. "I'm just sleepy," I said by way of explanation as I walked him to the front door.

"You're sure," he said.

"Yes, this has been great," I said.

"Good. So when can we meet again?" he asked. "I want to keep talking to you. I love practicing my English with you."

"Well, if we're going to do all this talking, I should be speaking in Spanish with you. It is the reason I'm here," I teased.

"Okay, we'll speak in Spanish half the time and then in English," Manuel offered.

I felt giddy with exhaustion and excitement. I liked this guy, and I thought he liked me, too. And there had been not a moment of sexual tension or innuendo. It seemed that Manuel just liked talking to me and I to him. What a refreshing concept.

"So how about tomorrow?" Manuel suggested.

I was about to say yes, but I remembered that Brook and I had promised Claudia to go with her on a field trip to Valladolid.

"I can't," I said, and Manuel actually looked wounded. "But what about Sunday?" I quickly countered.

We agreed to meet under the clock in the Plaza Mayor on Sunday at four o'clock for coffee and conversation.

"*Hasta pronto,*" Manuel said.

"*Hasta luego,*" I responded as I watched him disappear behind the elevator doors.

Manuel wasn't late on Sunday. I was. I saw him waiting under the clock tower, wearing his black and pink down parka, shivering in the still cold spring air. I ran up to him waving, suddenly feeling nervous and a little shy. We kissed on both cheeks to say hello and walked practically in silence to Salamanca's latest coffee bar/dance club, Cum Laude. Strategically built adjacent to the Plaza Mayor, the building blended in with the city's salmon-colored architecture. Inside, the walls were meant to resemble the ancient university buildings, complete with the busts of all of the great thinkers and philosophers carved into the stone. Only upon closer inspection, these busts weren't depictions of Aristotle and Plato, but rather Elton John and Madonna! I'd wanted to check the place out in the daytime, having only had a chance to experience Cum Laude's nighttime club scene.

Once inside the two-story building, we found a table upstairs, where it seemed to be quieter and more private. A mixture of Spanish and English Top 40 tunes played softly in the background. Right away I noticed that Manuel's eyes were actually green instead of brown, probably a reflection from the jade green cotton shirt he wore. I said this aloud and then practically bit my own tongue off for introducing body parts into our healthy, platonic new friendship. This was not supposed to be a romantic thing. But Manuel just took the comment as a comment and then suggested we place our orders. Without conferring we both ordered *café con leche*, which was served with a platter of exquisite little pastries.

"I love this," I gushed to Manuel. In my mind there was nothing better than a good cup of sweet milky coffee, pastries, and someone to talk to in a swank environment.

"Me, too," Manuel admitted.

We made ourselves comfortable, ignoring the occasional glares of the waiters who seemed perturbed that we weren't ordering more coffee. Like two nights before, once we started talking, we couldn't stop.

Manuel looked at his watch and started to laugh.

"You're not going to believe this," he said.

"Why, what time is it?" I asked.

"Guess," he teased.

"What, like six o'clock?" I asked in all seriousness.

"Actually it's nine twenty-five," he said, smiling.

I couldn't help myself and grabbed his wrist to look at his watch. How could five hours have passed without my noticing? It's not like we were talking about anything so profound. Just getting-to-know-you stuff—our favorite songs, the importance of our families, and what we wanted to be when we grew up. Surprisingly, we had many things in common. We both loved the band Toto, especially the song "Africa." Our families meant the world to us and neither one of us had a clear idea of what the future held in terms of career. I had come to Spain knowing I would revolutionize the system of public education in America, and now I wasn't so sure I wanted to be a public servant. Manuel was studying English because he loved languages, but he wasn't clear he really wanted to be a teacher in Spain. His family all had hopes that he would become a lawyer and take over his father's successful law practice.

"Oh, no," Manuel blurted out, with a panicked look on his face.

"What? What's the matter?" I asked.

"I've missed dinner at the dorm," he said, sounding like he had just missed his mother's funeral or something.

"Well, can't you eat out or something?" I suggested.

"I don't have any money," he said. "My parents send me an allowance to use, and it's gone. I just spent my last peseta on this coffee."

I had to laugh.

"Why are you laughing?" he asked me, looking a little put out.

"It's just that I'm in the exact same situation. I totally wanted to order another coffee, but I seriously don't have another penny."

"I hate depending on my parents for money," Manuel grumbled. "I can't wait to have my job and my own money."

"In the meantime," I said, "why don't you come to my apartment? At least I can feed you."

"That's okay," he said. "I have some secret cans of tuna stashed in my room. I can eat that."

Just the thought of Manuel trying to fill his stomach with contraband tuna made me sad, so I insisted. Besides, even though we'd spent the last five hours together, I wasn't ready to say good-bye.

Walking in the mostly deserted nighttime streets of Sally, Manuel and I laughed and joked and teased like old friends. I pointed out the tiny triangle of grass that I had dubbed Dogshit Park because of an unfortunate incident I'd had there in a pair of new shoes. He told me about his secret sadistic streak that made him want to just once drop-kick one of those ubiquitous little yip-yip dogs that seemed to think that Sally's sidewalks were a public doggie toilet. I laughed despite the fact that I love dogs. (The truth was, Salamanca did have a bit of a dogshit problem.) I couldn't erase the smile from my face. Manuel and I were real friends now, able to be honest and even a little bit gross without fear of offending the other. A barrier had been broken in those hours at Cum Laude. Once we made it to my apartment, I quickly became a Spanish woman, intent on feeding her man. (I was ecstatic that all three of my roommates were out.) With him seated in my tiny kitchen watching me cook, I whipped up the best meal I could, which turned out to be a simple French omelet and some slices of tomato drizzled with olive oil. I hoped this seemed better than tuna fish. He ate every bite and thanked me profusely. I felt a warm glow of satisfaction envelop me.

Like two nights before, after dinner we went into the salon. We sat down on the couch and continued talking, but this time something was different. I felt it. He felt it. There was electricity in the air. Little shocks of anticipation popped all over my body. I wanted him to kiss me so badly, I ached. But after an hour of flirtatious chatter and accidental touching, I remained unkissed. Finally, I couldn't hold myself back and I leaned over and kissed him. First on the forehead, then on each cheek, and finally lightly on the lips. And then he did the same back to me and the most delicious shiver traveled from the top of my head to the tips of my toes. And then we came together, kissing like we wanted to suck the essence out of each other. At some point we got up and opened the sofa into a bed, turned out the light, and closed the door. When the sun came up, we were still wrapped in each other's arms, still kissing and marveling in this feeling of completeness. We fell asleep, still in our clothing, me nestled under his arm.

In the morning when we woke, I was thankful my roommates were already gone, so I didn't have to explain Manuel in my bedroom. Until later. Manuel put his shoes back on and rearranged his clothes into some semblance of order. I tried to avert my eyes. A boy had never slept in my bed before. I wasn't sure of the protocol for such a situation. I tried to keep the tone in the room light and cheerful and devoid of expectations. I didn't want Manuel to feel obligated or responsible for my happiness. I walked him to the door and we said good-bye and that was that. I flew back to my room, jumped back in the bed, and fell asleep for four more hours.

Manuel showed up at my door the next afternoon completely unannounced to ask me if I wanted to take a walk. And I believe that's when I started to fall in love with him. It was such a simple gesture, but it was all I needed to know: that he wasn't just looking to score a piece of Black American ass. He really was interested in me. And though I had no experience in this arena, I think he wanted to be my *boyfriend*. And so for the rest of the year in Salamanca, the final three months, I did what I swore I wouldn't. I fell in love.

Manuel came over to our apartment almost every day, until Brook and Claudia started referring to him as the fifth roommate. His code name was Rupert, in case we wanted to talk about him in mixed company. Sometimes he slept over if he didn't want to make the long trek back to his dorm. Although I visited him there once, female visitors were not encouraged because his dorm doubled as a residence for young men entering the priesthood. I guess it was that man, woman, and Satan theory again.

The days passed entirely too fast, and Manuel and I fell into an easy familiarity where we simply avoided talking about the future. One afternoon while we were sitting on the steps of the university, playing our favorite game of "Guess where that *guiri* is from," Manuel made a confession.

"Before I met you," he started, "I didn't know if I could love anybody. I thought there might be something wrong with me because I never found anyone who I wanted to be with. You saved me," he said and laid his head down in my lap while I absorbed the weight of what he'd just said to me.

I stroked his thick head of curls and whispered back, "I love you, too."

I didn't know if this was the love I had always read about in my romance novels or the kind of love that lasts forever. But for the first time, I didn't really care. I promised simply to enjoy the here and now.

So when Manuel picked me up one evening and told me we were going to dinner with his best friend Nacho and we had to drive across
city lines to get there, I didn't ask questions, I simply grabbed my
purse and said, "Let's hit it."

My reward for being so relaxed and open-minded was the best
dinner I'd ever experienced in Spain. The restaurant in the town of
Zamora was actually a *bodega*, a real, working wine cellar that had
been partially converted into a dining space. I was skeptical as I
walked down the steep, dark staircase that looked like it descended
all the way to the pits of hell. But when we got to the bottom, although it was a bit dank, dark, and musty, it looked like a typical
Spanish restaurant with a bar and a handful of tables covered in
white linen tablecloths. I let Manuel and his friend Nacho order,
since they seemed to be relishing the role of tour guides. Taking my
cue from Nacho's beautiful girlfriend, María, I tried to sit back and
enjoy the experience. When the food came, I didn't have to try. We
started with a plate of homemade Manchego cheese, grilled chorizo
sausages, and rustic country bread. That was followed by a green
salad, a generous platter of the most amazing barbecued ribs flavored only with salt, pepper, and garlic, more bread, and a never-
ending pitcher of sweet, refreshing sangria. As I licked the grease
off my fingers I thought I had died and gone to heaven. The feeling
was mutual around the table.

By the time we were finished, all of us drunk on equal amounts of
grease, sangria, and laughter, it had been decided that the night was
too special to end. So we hopped in Nacho's little car and drove for the
rest of the night until we came to the northern coast of Spain, some
250 miles away from Salamanca. We watched the sun rise over the
Atlantic Ocean in a stunning display of yellow, oranges, and pinks.
I was delirious with lack of sleep and confused as to where we were,
but I knew I had never seen anything so perfectly gorgeous in my
entire life. It occurred to me at some point that I wasn't going to make
it to class that day, but school seemed so unimportant when Mother
Nature's majesty was shining before you.

Rather than ask Manuel and Nacho what was supposed to happen next, I just gave myself over to their whims. And so we spent the night at Nacho's parents' home in the town of Oviedo, which is where we had been heading all along. Oviedo is a beautiful northern city in the province of Asturias. Where Salamanca was all salmon-colored stone, Oviedo was vibrant, lush, and green.

The following day Nacho showed us around his hometown, including his favorite restaurant, where we ate mountains of fresh grilled seafood and washed it down with copious amounts of the region's famous, slightly alcoholic sparkly apple cider. As I sat in the booth alongside Manuel at the restaurant, nestled comfortably under his arm, a sigh escaped from my mouth.

"I don't want this day to end," I said.

"Me neither," Manuel said, squeezing my hand.

"You guys want to stay up here?" Nacho asked us. "We could open up a surf shop and become total surf bums." Nacho was already a major surfer and couldn't wait to be done with his studies in landlocked Salamanca.

María looked at her watch and became the voice of reason. "We have to head back because I have an exam tomorrow morning and I have to study."

We all groaned at that but knew our little escapade had come to an end.

And then the semester came to an end. I tried to come up with a way to stay in Salamanca for the summer, but it didn't make sense. Manuel would be in the south of Spain with his family, all of my friends would be gone, and the city would be inundated with foreigners trying to learn Spanish over the summer. Yuck. Salamanca was my city now. I didn't want to see her ravaged by opportunistic *guiris*.

Two nights before I left Salamanca, Manuel and I were sitting on my bed trying not to cry. Trying not to speak the obvious truth, that we'd probably never see each other again and that this sure had been fun while it lasted. It seemed unreal that this person whom I found it so easy to be with, this person who liked me as much as I liked him, wouldn't be in my world as soon as I stepped onto that airplane. But

another part of me, the part that watched my life unfold from a respectable distance, remembered that this was not real life. I had been
living a fantasy for the past nine months and playtime was over.

"You know I'd like to come visit you at Smith College," Manuel
said.

I tried to imagine a "boyfriend" brought back from my European
adventure like a souvenir. Imagining my Smith friends making fun of
me made me wrinkle my brow.

"That would be great," I said with fake enthusiasm. Manuel noticed.

"Well, I don't think I'd actually be able to travel until I finish here.
My parents would never pay for the ticket."

Even though he was a year older than I was, Manuel still had two
more years of college. So we were looking at two years before he'd
ever be able to visit. Just that thought of not seeing his beautiful face,
or being cuddled in his arms, or having him to talk to for two years
made my heart cave in with agony.

"We could get married," I blurted out without even thinking.

"No way," Manuel responded. "I'm not ready to marry you."

While I was happy that Manuel was being responsible, it still hurt
that he didn't want to get carried away with a dramatic, tear-jerking
scenario. I must have looked dejected, because Manuel opened his
arms to me.

"*Ven aquí,*" he said, and I crawled into those arms and he held me
there for the rest of the evening.

The two-hour drive to the Madrid airport in the middle of the night
was torturous. I cried big, hot tears the whole entire way, while Manuel, Nacho, and María tried to carry on a conversation that had nothing to do with me, or Manuel, or airports. Somewhere in the middle
of the journey Nacho stopped the car abruptly and ordered everyone
out of the vehicle. We seemed to be in the middle of nowhere. I didn't
see any other cars and it was so dark I could barely see my own hand
in front of me. I was really confused. I was so involved in my own misery and despair, perhaps I had missed something serious. Did we hit

an animal? Or maybe we were stopping for a group potty break, but I didn't need to pee. All of my excess bodily fluids had been cried out.

Nacho ushered us all toward the car's headlights so we could see. He cleared his throat in an obvious attempt to bring us to attention. Then he began to speak. He reminded me of our excellent adventure in Zamora, and of the formal dance I had attended at their dormitory, and of my disastrous attempt to make dinner for him at my apartment. He didn't stop talking until he had hilariously recaptured all of our great moments together. And then he thanked me for loving his good friend Manolo, whom he said he'd never seen happier. And this made me cry some more. Then he and María reached into the car and brought out a bag of parting gifts for me, which they presented one by one. First, a big green boomerang to remind me to come back to Spain. Next, a cassette tape of Spanish guitar legend Paco de Lucía to remind me to keep playing my guitar. And finally a Spanish cookbook. In it, they had inscribed: *"Recuerda las tapas y las copas que tomabas en España. Ya sabes que a los españoles, sobre todo al tuyo, se les conquista por el estómago."* (Remember all of the tapas and drinks you had in Spain. Now you know that Spaniards, especially your Spaniard, are conquered through their stomachs.) My tears doubled in intensity. I was so touched by these thoughtful gifts and so sad that I was leaving when it seemed I had finally found my happiness in Spain. I couldn't stop crying until I was on the airplane. (I probably would have cried even more if I had known that Nacho, despite his jovial exterior, was suffering from severe depression and would take his own life three years later.) I ached with longing for Manuel and for Spain, but I knew my parenthesis from reality was over. It was time for me to get back to life.

🖋 11 : *La Reconquista*

I couldn't eat. I left my appetite in Spain. In my journal I wrote, "The pain of starvation is preferable to the pain of remembering." Somehow I had placed all my memories and my love of Spain and of Manuel in my stomach. The pleasure of eating would be a betrayal somehow. So I didn't eat. The food my mother set before me didn't even tempt me.

"You better eat something before I have you committed to a mental institution," my mother threatened. She had come to the end of her tolerance for my dramatic transition back into American life. It had been a week since I had returned home from Europe. I was weepy, didn't talk much, and spent a great deal of time in my room playing the guitar and writing really bad poetry in Spanish and English.

"Why should I eat," I responded, "when I have nothing to eat for?"

My mother rolled her eyes and tried really hard not to slap me back into shape.

"Here's something you need to eat for," she said instead. "You need to eat so you'll have enough energy to get a job so you can pay us back some of the money we just spent on you to have your European experience and so you can go back to Smith with some money in your pocket. How about that for a reason to eat?"

"I was thinking about getting an internship," I said to my mother.

"Will you make any money?" my mother asked, cutting to the chase.

"Don't you want to know what kind of internship I'm thinking about?" I queried.

My mother sighed. She was used to my "guess what I'm going to be when I grow up" ideas that changed quite frequently. Before I had settled on teacher, being a midwife, innkeeper, actress, and veterinarian had all been serious considerations.

"What? What are you thinking about now?" Mom asked with a sigh of resignation.

"I want to get an internship at a magazine, because I want to see if magazine journalism is the kind of writing I want to do," I said. "I really want to be a writer, which means I may have to change my major at Smith to English, which means I might have to stay one more semester."

My mother looked at me like she wanted to choke the life out of me. When she spoke, though, her voice was very calm. This was a technique she'd perfected working with crazy people for a living.

"Lori, you can get whatever internship you want. But if it doesn't pay, you better get a real job as well. A real full-time job. And you will not change your major because I will not be paying for a fifth year of Smith College. No way! You will finish your degree in education, because no matter what you finally decide you want to do, you will always be able to have teaching to fall back on. End of story."

"You know, Mom," I said, trying to sound worldly and wise, "work isn't everything. That's what's wrong with American society. In Europe people believe you have to find your passion in life or else what's the point?"

"I didn't say you shouldn't follow your dreams, Lori," my mother countered. "I just said you have to get a job that pays you money this summer. Sometimes passion requires sacrifice. If working at a magazine is something you really want to do, then you shouldn't mind putting in the extra time to work there and get a paying job, too."

I didn't have an answer for that. I knew I needed the money, but I was desperate to see if I could make a career out of writing. In Spain, with all of that time on my hands to reflect and really get to know myself, I realized that I'd always wanted to write and owed it to myself to pursue that dream. Like the Europeans in Spain who were there to pursue their love of a language. Not because it would advance their careers, but because they derived pleasure from rolling *r*'s and lisping *c*'s. Because the smell of garlic and olive oil made their mouths water. Because taking a nap in the middle of the day sounded like heaven. I wanted to pursue writing not because it would look good on a résumé or make me rich and powerful. Writing made me happy. It was that simple. So I was determined to do whatever it took to make my happiness real. I wasn't afraid to sacrifice. But it was true, I needed to prove to myself that this "writing is my life" decision was going to stick.

By the middle of June, I was eating again. Through sheer luck I managed to score an internship at Milwaukee's only legitimate glossy, *Milwaukee Magazine.* They actually had an official internship program and the person who had been selected for the position had backed out at the last minute, leaving the door wide open for *moi.* I worked at the magazine three afternoons a week, worked as a secretary in an accountant's office around those hours, and babysat on the weekends for every kid under age ten on my parents' block. It didn't take long for Spain to seem like a lazy dream I had had years ago.

Sometimes the taste of a pungent green olive or the smell of fresh garlic could carry me back to Salamanca, but I was now ready to get serious and focus on the future. I had expunged my Spanish fantasy from my system. My year in Spain had been a fantastic experience, but now I knew for sure that it would never live up to my childhood dreams. Spain hadn't embraced me, hadn't welcomed me with open arms and allowed me to forget about the color of my skin. If anything, being in Spain had made me more aware of being Black, but that wasn't a bad thing, I realized, because once I got past the irritating stares and comments, I was allowed to redefine Black for the Spaniards who really cared to listen and learn. But like Morocco, Spain would be catalogued under "amazing learning experience," demoted from "the place that would change my life and possibly where I'd like to live."

The constant stream of letters from Manuel was the only real connection I had to Spain, and I figured eventually they, too, would stop. But for now they arrived quite regularly—long pages of chatter written in Spanish and English and often accompanied by random doodles and silly cartoon faces. I read each letter, giggling at this silly boy who wrote with the same humor and openness he showed in person. Reading Manuel's letters was like having a conversation with him—he sometimes even scribbled in my responses. I carried each letter to my room, read it several times, and then placed it in a special basket with the others. When I collected five, I'd tie them up with multicolored ribbons, storing them like precious souvenirs. With each passing day, even with his letters and the letters I wrote back to him, Manuel too began to feel like a souvenir, like something I could wrap up and put away. Eventually I assumed that, like Quique, Manuel would find someone else nearby to love and the letters would stop coming. Only this time I would be prepared.

In the meantime, I was loving my internship at the magazine. In between fact-checking riveting articles on feng shui and the proper way to make a real Wisconsin cream puff, I was helping an associate editor uncover a heinous medical con game. The ringleader was a charlatan M.D. who claimed that most people's chronic pain came from tooth decay. So along with his slimy partners he'd duped dozens of people into getting their teeth pulled to relieve their back pain. Most of the victims were elderly. I got to interview the patients who were filing a class-action lawsuit, learned how to procure legal documents from the courthouse, and even got to pose as a patient to see if this guy was still trying to scam people (he was). At home, I threw all my energies into helping my mom plan for her family reunion, slated for the Fourth of July weekend. My mother was one of eleven siblings, so when the whole clan made a promise to get together, it was a big deal. While the majority of my aunties lived in Milwaukee, the remaining four or five were scattered across the United States, from Buffalo to Atlanta. Even my sister planned to fly in from Brussels. I couldn't wait because every time my mother's family got together, the combination of good food, bellyaching laughs, and the opportunity to see my mother act like a naughty schoolgirl with her sisters was priceless. There was probably no better way to complete my reacculturation to America then by being surrounded by my mother's rambunctious, fun-loving family.

• • •

The phone was ringing but I didn't bother to answer it. Nine months living without a telephone in Spain made it easy to ignore the persistent ring. Besides, someone else would probably get it. Anyway, the calls were rarely for me at my parents' home anymore.

My mother came rushing into the family room, where I was splayed out on the couch reading. "Lori, it's him," she whispered, clutching the phone to her bosom. I knew that meant Manuel, but I couldn't figure out my mother's air of urgency. It was as if just because the call came from overseas, she got hysterical. She handed me the cordless phone and watched me like a hawk. I took the phone and walked away from her prying eyes and ears and headed back to my bedroom.

"¿Sí?" I said into the phone, nervous for no good reason.

"Lori?" Manuel said like a question.

"Sí. Hola." I waited for him to start the conversation. Even though we never ran out of things to talk about in person, the telephone always made communication seem stilted and dry. We hadn't spoken on the phone since I left Spain.

Without preamble or warm-up, Manuel said he wanted to come to Milwaukee.

"I have a friend in Salamanca whose father arranges for Spanish students to come to the States to babysit or help in the house somehow to help practice their English . . . she says he might know some people in Milwaukee but he's not sure . . . but I thought your mother might know a family who might want a Spanish student." All of this came out as one long, hopeful sentence.

It was true I had mentioned that my mother was still the home-stay coordinator for AFS at University School, but I didn't think Manuel would remember that random fact I'd mentioned at some point in our relationship.

"And when do you want to come?" I asked, as I tried to imagine Manuel in Milwaukee. I couldn't see it. It seemed too far-fetched.

"As soon as possible. I already asked my father for the ticket and he said yes, so I just have to find a family. Do you think you could ask your mother if she knows someone?"

For some reason this request irritated me. Manuel was neatly packed away in the fond-memories pile of my mind and now he wanted to unpack himself? Rather than exploring this emotion, I just got a little snippy and lied a little bit.

"I don't think my mom knows any families interested in a summer student. She pretty much only works with people who want a high school student for the year."

"Well, could you ask her anyway? She might know something," Manuel said, sounding somewhere between really desperate and really eager, which made me really mad. How dare he interrupt my well-ordered reality?

"Sure, I'll ask her," I said, even though in my head I was thinking I'd do no such thing. My mother probably had no interest in bringing the little Spanish boy I had a fling with on my junior year abroad into her world or back into mine.

We hung up soon after and I shook my head at the thought of Manuel coming here to my piece of suburban America. He'd probably hate it. But really there was something else holding me back. Just like back when the Spaniards came to my high school, I had this immediate knee-jerk desire to keep Manuel from seeing what Black really meant in America. What I feared was that when Manuel saw how Black people were treated here, how the Black people were portrayed in the media and on the news, and even how we treated one another, he'd decide he wanted nothing to do with me. While I was in Spain, I'd been able to define Black any way I wanted to because there weren't enough people to contradict me. Although the term "exotic" rankled me in Spain, at least I got to define Black for myself. In Spain I didn't carry the stigma of "welfare-queen, ghetto bitch, ignorant, criminal-minded minority." If Manuel came here to segregated Milwaukee—or anywhere in the United States—he'd watch the news and see the inner city and witness the public's general disrespect for my people and discover there was nothing exotic about me. He'd realize I was just one of a group of a historically oppressed people. And with that knowledge he might not want to be associated with me and mine. I didn't want to go there. I wanted Manuel and me to stay a sweet, simple romance that happened on my junior year abroad. A story to tell and a bittersweet memory to linger over when I felt lonely and misunderstood.

I walked back into the family room, where my mother looked like she was about to jump out of her chair.

"So, what did he want?" she asked me, trying to keep her voice neutral.

"Nothing, really," I said, struggling with my conscience. I really didn't think my mother had any families that fit the bill, but even if she did, I didn't think she'd want to take a chance on some random guy, even if he had been someone special to me. But then my inner Malcolm X (I had finished reading his autobiography in Spain) pushed me to be honest. I had no right to hide my people from the rest of the world. I needed to stop trying to downplay the Black side of myself and raise it up for applause, since there was much to be proud of. It was hard for me, though, after years of keeping the Negro in me quietly in the corner. A tiny Black fist raised itself somewhere in my chest.

"So he just called to say hi?" my mother asked, sounding suspicious.

"Actually," I said, "he wanted to know if you could find him a family to live with over the summer, so he can come here and practice his English. Can you believe that?" I gave an incredulous laugh, hoping she'd agree that it was an audacious and ludicrous request. But she didn't.

"You know, I have the perfect family," my mom said, jumping up and running to her desk in the kitchen. In what seemed like a split second she'd located her notebook, dialed three or four different numbers, and then turned to me and said, "Okay, I got the family. When does he want to start?"

The fact that "the perfect family" lived across the street from us always seems like something I engineered when I tell this story, but I swear I had nothing to do with it. I couldn't believe that my Spanish love story was going to have another chapter here in my hometown. Manuel was on his way to work as an au pair in exchange for room and board with the family who lived across the street from my parents. I had to pick him up from the airport and bring him to my home, where he'd stay for the weekend before meeting his new employers. Of course this was the weekend of the big reunion, so my entire extended family was waiting back at the house to pounce on Lori's new boyfriend. "Leave it to Lori to bring a foreigner to the family reunion," I'm sure all my relatives were saying to one another. In my greater extended family, I was known as the eccentric one, likely to do or try anything as long as it was weird and unexpected.

It was July third and I was watching the fireworks as I drove my little white Ford Festiva to the airport. I wondered if Manuel would look any different. I wondered if I still loved him. A million thoughts and emotions raced through my body. Excitement. Fear. Anxiety. And just a little bit of joy. To quell the firestorm, I just told myself that first and foremost, Manuel was my friend and I would treat him like a good friend visiting the States for the first time. Like any of our other AFS students, I'd show him the sights and sounds of Milwaukee. That sounded like a workable plan. Manuel, friend. Me, tour guide.

Manuel had called earlier from New York. Somehow he had managed to buy a ticket only from Madrid to New York and was trying to figure out how to get a ticket to Milwaukee, which required getting from JFK International Airport to LaGuardia Airport on a bus through Queens. It didn't help that his textbook English was pretty useless in real-life situations. He gave me the information for the flight he intended to be on and I prayed he would make it without incident.

I parked the car in the lot at the airport. I was alone by choice. I didn't want anyone around for our reunion. I didn't know what to expect. I was nervous and I was sweating profusely. I made it inside and checked the arrivals board and saw that his flight was about to land. I went right to the gate and tried to figure out where I could stand so I would see him first and he wouldn't see me. I didn't have long to wait. The plane must have already been there. I spotted Manuel's coat first. Leave it to Manuel, who always hated cold weather, to wear his down parka in the middle of the summer. He saw me then and practically crushed me in an embrace that conveyed his happiness and relief, his long journey over. In his arms again, I felt a rush of emotion so strong it almost knocked the wind out of me.

During the ride back home Manuel recapped his sixty-hour journey from the south of Spain to Milwaukee. The story was fraught with missteps and near misses, but here he was, safe and sound. I was only half listening, though. I was taking stock of this Spanish man-child and trying to see what my family would see. Under his parka, Manuel was wearing the typical Spanish uniform of jeans and a black T-shirt. The jeans and the T-shirt were ironed; the shirt was tucked in and held in place with a leather belt. Black dress shoes covered his feet. His clothes weren't what I was afraid my family would notice first. It was his incredibly pale skin and skinny body. It wasn't like we didn't have White spouses scattered across our family tree, and just because my mother and her sisters all struggled with obesity didn't mean they couldn't love skinny people. It was just that Manuel looked so glaringly opposite to what was familiar. I feared my family might not know what to do with him. I started to warn Manuel of each relative's peculiarities but then decided it was best not to make him too afraid. I just hoped for the best. Truth be told, I wanted to see if Manuel could survive my crazy relatives. Lesser men who considered English their mother tongue had been known to flee in horror after attending a Fourth of July or Memorial Day picnic with the Bradford clan. I didn't know if this lightweight foreigner would be up to the task.

I took a deep breath when we walked in the front door. I prayed that the roomful of people I had left behind when I left for the airport might have dispersed, but they hadn't. In fact, every last one of them had claimed a seat in my parents' great room, and they were all quietly sitting there in a circle, looking like some official tribunal waiting to try their first case. I plunged right into the middle of the circle, dragging Manuel behind me, and made the introductions.

"Everybody, this is Manuel," I said. "Manuel, this is . . ." and I went around the circle, starting with my parents, and named names. Of course my mother made a speech of welcome and then everyone else just said hi, until we got to my uncle Kevin, who can never do things normally. I worried what he was going to say to embarrass Manuel.

"Come here," he said to Manuel, who had remained in the middle of the circle, looking very much like a deer caught in the headlights of an eighteen-wheeler.

Manuel went and stood in front of my uncle Kevin, who made a show of looking Manuel up and down like he was checking out a new car. Manuel appeared to be in pain.

"Aww, I'm just kidding," Kevin laughed, and embraced Manuel in one of those Black man hugs that looks solid and loving at the same time. Manuel hugged him right back. And then everyone started laughing and being loud and I exhaled.

"I love your family," Manuel told me two nights later. We'd been doing nonstop family activities, interspersed with my trying to show Manuel the sights and sounds of Milwaukee. The next morning he would meet his host family across the street. This was the last night he would be snuggled up on the pullout sofa in my parents' family room.

"They seem to love you, too," I said. I didn't want to say it out loud, but I was so impressed at how comfortable Manuel appeared with my people. Every gathering was always loud and crowded, with no rhyme or reason. We'd just go from house to house, eating, laughing, and telling stories and dirty jokes. Manuel would always just find a place to take it all in, laughing with the rest of us. My uncle Kevin asked him once, "Do you understand all this trash people are talking about?"

And Manuel responded honestly: "No."

"Then why are you laughing?" Kevin asked.

"Because you guys are having so much fun I just can't help but laugh, too."

It had been decided, before everyone returned to their respective homes, that Manuel could be an honorary member of the family.

"I don't want to go live with another family," Manuel admitted, getting cozy under the covers of his lumpy sofa bed. "I wish I could just stay here," he said.

I stroked his curly hair and admonished him, "You'd get sick of us sooner or later and you'll learn more English over there because they don't speak a word of Spanish." I didn't mention that I didn't want him in my home for the summer, that I wanted some distance (even if it was only the street) between us so I could make sure my feelings for him were real and lasting. What if I found out I hated him and he was stuck in our house? I was getting a painful Craig the Smellyman flashback. Even across the street would be too close if that happened.

"I could never get sick of your family. I love them so much," he assured me.

"You'll be so proud of yourself, and think of how much English you'll learn," I said, willing him to take the hint that we should have some space between us before we lived together, even it was only for a month. "Besides, we'll be right across the street, so you can come over anytime you want," I added, to give him something to hold on to.

And that's exactly what he did.

That summer became a pattern of me trudging off to one of my two jobs and then getting home at 6:30 or 7:00 p.m., exhausted. As if he had been waiting to hear the sound of my little car rolling into the driveway, Manuel would appear at our door three seconds later. He was so desperate to get away from the three demonic children and overly chatty mother at the house across the street, he sometimes made it to my house before I did, perfectly content to chitchat with my mom over tea. Both of us weary by the evening, Manuel and I fell into a pretty boring routine of hanging out with my parents, watching TV, and eating dinner together, followed by sessions of heavy petting somewhere in the great outdoors near my house. On the weekends, we'd do tourist things like visit museums or catch the train to Chicago so Manuel could see a *real* American city. The whole time, though, we never talked about our future. It was like I was trying out a new sweater, this Manuel. What did it feel like to have a White-looking, Spanish-speaking significant other in my world? He'd won over my entire extended family, securing his place when he gobbled up a plate of pig's feet and chitterlings without a grimace and actually asked for seconds. Now he just had to pass my tests.

So far, I'd endured no painful recriminations from the Angry Black Man (or Woman) about our being together. As the summer came to a close, I realized the only person holding me back from loving this Spaniard who seemed to be entirely devoted to me was me. And that's when my heart melted. Two days before he was due to leave, I fell in love again. This time for real, no fantasies involved. He passed the test and I knew we could really be a couple. A forever-and-ever couple. And then I remembered that he didn't live in the same country and that we both had to finish college and that there were so many obstacles barring our happily ever after. Just the kind of perfect drama I'd always read about. So while I was wailing on the outside over the injustice of finally finding my Prince Charming, like the kid who can't stop poking that painful part of the gum where the tooth has fallen out, I took some freakish delight at the circumstances of my now-official long-distance, star-crossed romance.

❧ 12: Guess Who's Coming to *la Cena*?

It took a long time for the smell of Thai yellow curry and jasmine rice to stop making me sick. I had worked for exactly three weeks as a waitress at a Thai restaurant in Northampton in order to pay for my ticket back to Spain. The work was painful under the sadistic eye of Nok, the restaurant owner, who made Attila the Hun seem like a nice person. If we didn't say thank you, in Thai, to the cooks every time we picked up an order, she'd slap our hands with a metal spatula. She loved to bark orders at us and call us stupid for not being able to say things in Thai. And then, just to keep us reeling, she'd make us all eat dinner together family style after the restaurant closed. And it wasn't rare for her to suggest that we all, family style, cram into her minivan and road-trip to Boston in the middle of the night.

I endured it all, including the traditional Thai outfit she tried to make me wear, even though my very African booty protested greatly in the narrow skirt. All for love. Manuel and I had managed to stay grotesquely in love (according to my friends) and in debt (transatlantic phone calls and airmail stamps add up) for the months after he left Milwaukee. It wasn't hard. We were both heavily involved in our studies and used to being alone. I had all my girlfriends for companionship, and Manuel's regular letters and occasional phone calls kept my heart happy. For the first time in my college career I didn't hate the post office. It was now a source of great happiness, because a letter from Manuel arrived regularly with detailed updates on his life and passions. Including his ever-growing infatuation with Michael Jordan. Likewise, I regaled him with all of the goings-on of my friends' nervous breakdowns, falls off the wagon, acceptances to graduate school, and, like mine, general anxiety about The Future. I secured an internship at a local magazine in Northampton and it was becoming very clear that I wanted to work as a journalist, but I wasn't sure I had the requisite talent. All of this I dumped on Manuel, and he'd patiently write back words of encouragement and support.

So far, our long-distance relationship was working just fine. Manuel had come back to Milwaukee to visit over Christmas, so it was my turn now to go back to Spain. Spring break was my goal. My parents had no problem with my plans, but they made it perfectly clear that they wouldn't be contributing to my European travel fund. Thus the waitressing job. As soon as I had the money for the ticket, I happily told Nok I quit and tossed my curry-scented uniform into a garbage bin in the alley. Cash in hand, I booked my ticket the next day—a round trip from Boston to Madrid. Manuel was going to meet me in Madrid, we'd take the bus to Salamanca, and then he was going to plan a special weekend trip for us to take before we headed south, where I was going to meet his family.

Strolling through the streets of Salamanca, holding hands with Manuel, it felt like I'd never left. Nothing had changed in this ancient city in the year I'd been gone. There was a new crop of international students greedily gobbling up the city's charms. The ratio of nightclubs to students remained ridiculously high. And yes, the dogshit still liberally dotted the sidewalks. It was good to be back.

I wanted to stop and see my old apartment, my favorite shoe store, and El Puerto de Chus. I wanted to visit Hermi and the IES director, Daniel Pastor, who coincidentally happened to be one of Manuel's favorite English professors at the university. We thought he'd get a kick out of our romance, since I had become one of his program pets in my last semester, hanging out at the IES office, offering to do odd jobs, and sometimes just shooting the breeze with his wife, Concha.

"What do you think Daniel's going to say when he finds out we're together?" I asked Manuel, still not believing I was back.

"No sé," Manuel answered distractedly. He was a little nervous just dropping in on a professor. This was Spain, after all, where authority figures were still people to be feared and revered, not dropped in on for a "Hey, guess who my girlfriend is?" social call. Before I could reassure Manuel that Daniel seemed to be a very friendly man who I was sure wouldn't fault him for an unannounced visit, I screamed and tried to hide behind Manuel.

"¿Qué pasa?" Manuel said, looking around for the source of my distress.

I unclenched my eyes and peeked around Manuel to see if in fact I saw what I thought I had seen. And indeed, marching straight toward us down the street was what looked to be a parade of the Ku Klux Klan in white hoods. Maybe things had changed since I'd been gone. The Klan had come to Spain.

"What are they doing here?" I croaked to Manuel, while trying to pull him out of view of the slowly marching Klan. I noticed that everyone else on the street was stopping to watch their progression. Maybe they were as scared as I was. I wasn't sure if the Klan liked Spaniards, but I was pretty sure they were anti-Catholic, so that didn't bode well for 99 percent of the people on the street with me.

Manuel turned to look at me like I was crazy. "That's a *procesión*. They're marching for Semana Santa," he said.

"Why are they wearing Klan hoods?" I demanded, feeling sheepish but angry just the same. How could anyone wear that getup with impunity in today's world?

Apparently Manuel knew what the KKK was without my explaining. "Um, I think the church had the hoods first and the KKK stole the idea."

"Yeah, but still. I don't care if Jesus Christ himself is under one of those things, it's scary for a Black person to see a bunch of hooded men coming toward her," I said in my own defense.

"Well, it's just tradition," Manuel said. "They march every year for Semana Santa and sometimes the hoods are different colors. They're not always white."

I didn't know if that bit of information was supposed to make me feel better, or if Manuel was just sharing knowledge. Either way, it just made me feel that Spain really wasn't a country where a Black girl would ever feel at home.

Portugal, on the other hand, felt like a dream. There were palm trees, lush beaches, and enough Black people in the mix to make me just one more. Incognegro on the Iberian Peninsula at last. The brown-skinned people in Portugal were mostly immigrants from the Cape Verde Islands, but they'd been in the country for generations and considered themselves Portuguese. I also saw Indians (from Goa) and a fair number of Asians walking the streets of Lisbon. I didn't inquire much about Portuguese racial politics during our weekend trip, but I felt immediately at ease in the crowds of rainbow-hued citizens.

Manuel had booked our minivacation in the luxe resort town of Cascais, right outside of Lisbon. We stayed at a swank hotel where we did nothing but eat, swim in the pool, spend a lot of time in bed, take walks on the beach, and eat some more. Manuel had splurged and recklessly spent his entire month's allowance on this one weekend. I knew I ought to feel guilty, but I didn't. Not one little bit.

"I could live here forever," I moaned in absolute ecstasy as I sunned myself on a giant rock in the shadow of the ocean.

"What about Spain?" Manuel asked, watching me from his own rock.

Without thinking, I sighed, "I don't think so."

I didn't notice the disappointment all over Manuel's face when I said that because I was too busy soaking up the Portuguese sun, which just felt so much warmer than anything I had recently experienced in blustery, cold, western Massachusetts.

Manuel stayed silent, so I finally turned away from the sun and tried changing the subject.

"So tell me about your family again. What do you think they're going to think of me?"

In general I held a pretty high opinion of myself and believed if people didn't like me, then it was because there was something wrong with them, not me. I knew myself to be personable, friendly, a good conversationalist, and an all-around people person. Sure, after you get to know me really well, you may find some of my habits annoying, but first impressions I generally nailed. But meeting Manuel's family had me doubting my own abilities to impress. This was Spain, after all, where I had already ascertained that Black women weren't regarded as quality girlfriend material, at least from a parent's point of view. And who knows what other ideas they might have picked up from Hollywood or the American news media about Black Americans in general. Add to that the fact that Manuel's family lived in a small fishing village so far south in Spain, the lights from the Moroccan highways could be seen from the beaches. And everybody knows that the small-town mentality means new people are not generally wanted. Especially new people who look different.

"They are going to love you as much as I do," Manuel said. "Especially my sister." Manuel's sister was eight years his junior, and there was a mutual admiration society between the two of them. She was clearly his favorite sibling.

"What about your parents?" I queried, because truth be told it was their opinion that mattered most.

Manuel hesitated for a moment too long before he answered and I pounced.

"What?"

"Nothing." He tried to shrug it off.

"Not nothing, you were going to say something. What? What about your parents?"

"Well, it's just that none of my brothers have ever brought a girl over before, so this is kind of a big deal. Plus you're staying at the house."

"I thought both of your brothers had girlfriends," I said.

"They do," Manuel said.

"And they've never been to your house?" I asked, thinking I must have misunderstood something.

"Nope. In Spain you don't bring your girlfriends over unless it is really serious."

"So then are they going to think we're really serious?" I asked, not sure if that was a good assumption (meaning I'm important) or a bad assumption (meaning this chick is going to steal our son and take him back to America).

"Well, they might," Manuel said.

I groaned. "Well, then, I shouldn't be staying in your house. I should find a hotel to stay in or something."

"There are no hotels in Barbate," he said, laughing at the idea.

"Well, I don't want them to think too much of this. I mean, it's not like you're bringing me home to marry me . . ." I left a pause here in case Manuel wanted to do something dramatic and romantic and propose right here on this blessed piece of Portuguese paradise. But he didn't.

"Don't worry, *hija*," he said. "They understand that you're my friend and you're visiting me from the States and you have to stay in our house 'cause where else would you stay? I mean, when Nacho and María came down they stayed with us, too."

"Okay," I said, relaxing a bit. But then I remembered one more thing. "But what about the Black thing? Do they find Black women as appealing as you do?"

Manuel shrugged his shoulders. "They won't care. They'll just think you're beautiful," he said, leaning over to kiss the tip of my nose. "But you know, it's funny," he said, shaking his head.

"What? What's funny?" I asked.

"When I was little, I used to torment my grandfather by telling him I was going to marry a Black woman when I grew up. And he'd go crazy."

I was finding this strange, not funny.

"What do you mean?" I asked.

"Well, my grandfather used to always say that the races shouldn't mix. That Black should stay with Black and White with White, so to make him angry I'd tell him I was going to marry a Black woman. And sometimes my little brother Agu would egg him on, saying, 'Manolo is going to marry a Black woman! Manolo is going to marry a Black woman!' and my grandfather would just start yelling at us."

"Is that a normal threat for Spanish children to make, to threaten to marry a Black person?" I had to ask.

"No, it was just something I did," Manuel clarified. "I just thought it was stupid what he said, so to make him mad I'd say that. But I've always fantasized about marrying a foreigner. Probably a beautiful, blond, tall German type," he said.

I fell for that and smacked him for the audacity. Manuel just laughed. "I'm just kidding, honey bunny," he said. Manuel loved to try out American terms of endearment on me.

"So, am I going to meet this grandfather?" I asked, knowing that most of Manuel's relatives lived in Barbate, save an aunt in Málaga and some wayward cousins in Mexico.

"Of course," Manuel said, as if the question were ridiculous.

"Well, is he going to spit on me or something?" I asked in all seriousness.

"Titi," he said, resorting to our own personal term of endearment, "my grandfather will love you. He's not racist. He just doesn't know any better. He's never even met any Black people. And I told him all about you."

"Great," I said and vowed not to think about the Malia clan until I absolutely had to.

He was waiting for me to laugh. In a split-second decision that I knew my fate depended on, I ignored my politically correct training, my solidarity with my brown brothers and sisters and everything I knew to be right and true, and I laughed. I laughed at the joke where the punch line was an off-color comment about Chinese people. I laughed because, thankfully, the punch line wasn't about Black people. And I laughed because it was Manuel's eighty-year-old grandfather telling me the joke, as a way of welcoming me to his home and into the family, and the thought that this joke was supposed to put me at ease was in fact actually quite hilarious. But apparently it did the trick, because once Abuelo and I were yukking it up together, everybody else gave an audible sigh of relief that we could all get along. There we were, Manuel, me, his maternal grandparents, his mother, and a random cousin or two standing in front of the grandparents' home. I had only been in Barbate for about ten minutes, and the first hurdle was passed.

Now we had to go meet the rest of Manuel's immediate family. Manuel's mother had picked us up from the bus station and brought us immediately to meet her parents. They lived precisely two minutes by car from Manuel's home. So I didn't have long to prepare myself for the next meeting.

The house Manuel grew up in, unlike his grandparents', which was a classic Spanish *casa blanca* with a red terra-cotta roof and a riot of colorful blossoms all around, was more of a town house. He lived in the "city" in a space that would be considered woefully small for a family of six by American standards. But in the town of Barbate, Manuel's family was considered upper middle class. When I entered the house, the lime green walls and cool marble floors immediately made me think of the Spain of my imagination. When we reached the second floor and slid open the pocket doors, I knew exactly how Manuel had felt last summer in my home. The rest of the family was sitting in the salon, apparently waiting for my arrival. Manuel's older brother, Juan, whom I had met briefly in Salamanca, jumped up to greet me. "Loli!" he cried, kissed me on both cheeks and then enveloped me in a reassuring hug. Manuel's mother, Elisa, then took over introductions and introduced me to her husband, Juan, her daughter, Eli (short for Elisa), and her other son, Agustín, Manuel's younger brother. They all seemed to eye me warily. Or was I just imagining things? I sat down in an offered chair and tried to answer the questions lobbed at me but had a bit of a hard time understanding their thick southern accents. I think I came off as either aloof or retarded. Manuel just watched the whole thing unfold. I felt especially bad when Elisa told me she'd heard I loved sweets and then passed a plate of cookies that were native to their town. *"Son muy ricas,"* she said, offering me the plate. They didn't look like cookies exactly and so I asked what the little nutlike things poking out of what appeared to be a caramel glaze were.

"Piñones," she said, smiling at me.

I turned to Manuel for a quick translation.

"Pine nuts," he said. And I wanted to cry. There are very few things

I won't eat in this world. Pine nuts are high on the list, though. Right after beets. Just the thought of them makes my tongue twist. But I didn't want to be rude on my first visit, so I took a cookie and tried to take bites so tiny I wouldn't be able to taste the nuts. I didn't fool anyone.

"You don't like them," his mother said.

"No, not really," I admitted, wondering if I had sealed my fate with those words.

"No pasa nada," his mother said, but I swore she was thinking "ungrateful bitch."

The rest of the time we all sat in mostly uncomfortable silence and I wondered what had happened to that Manuel who had sat at my dinner table in Salamanca and had been able to keep the conversation flowing between the most dissimilar party guests. He was nowhere to be found. This Manuel sat aligned with his family and watched us all not really talking. I willed coffee hour to be over soon.

Afterward, Manuel gave me a tour of the rest of the house. It seemed worn and lived in, complete with posters of Johnny Depp in Eli's room and Pamela Anderson on the walls of Agu's room. Manuel dragged me up to the roof of the house, also known as the patio. From up there I could see the whole city of Barbate.

"We used to keep our dogs up here," Manuel said, pointing to a small shedlike structure where the dogs used to sleep. "Now my cousin Paco uses that space for a darkroom. He loves to take pictures."

That reminded me. I was taking Photography 101 during my last semester at Smith. It was my attempt at getting an artsy course in before I graduated. I seemed to have a good eye for taking pictures but was too lazy to keep my camera with me all the time. But I did have it now, and the view from the rooftop was amazing, so I started shooting. Soon Manuel's brothers and sister joined us, and somehow mugging in front of my lens, we broke through all that formality from downstairs. By dinnertime, I was an accepted guest, the preferred target for teasing and tormenting with strange foodstuffs. By the time I fell asleep that night in the twin bed Manuel had slept in as a child, I felt accepted by the entire Malia clan. Even his father, who treated me like I was hearing impaired, speaking to me in an extra-loud tone of voice with wild, overly exaggerated hand signals, seemed to give me the proverbial thumbs-up.

"Shit. Shit. Shit." I hated my hair.

Manuel knocked on the door again, and again I said through gritted teeth, "I'm coming."

I surveyed the mess on the bathroom floor, in the sink, and even all over the walls. After a vigorous session of blow-drying, my hair was back to its bone-straight state, but there were also thick black strands covering the entire room. This always happened when I dried my hair; it was part of the process of being beautiful in an assimilated kind of way. For me to maintain the appearance of having silky-smooth straight hair, I had to burn the kinks out, first with chemicals, then with hot air. A small price to pay, I always thought, until now. As I surveyed the damage I felt a sheet of shame rising in my body. How was I supposed to explain this mess to my hosts? Not to mention the distinctive odor of burning hair. And if I asked for a broom, they'd probably say don't worry about it, then come and see the mess and recoil in horror and forbid their son from socializing ever again with a freak like me. I wanted to cry.

Finally I stuck my head out of the door and called for Manuel. He'd have to be my confidant here. Luckily he came quickly to the bathroom door. I asked him to get me a broom and a plastic bag. I didn't want any evidence of my hair left behind, not even in the garbage can. Manuel brought me a broom and I swept all the hair up, wiped it from the tile walls and bathroom sink with wads of toilet paper, and shoved it all into the plastic grocery bag. Now they'd be none the wiser that (a) after a shower my hair kinks back up, and (b) to get it straight I have to rip half of it out. My secret was safe.

We were supposed to be going out to dinner to celebrate my last night with the family. Even though I was sure to come home reeking of cigarette smoke, I made sure to shower before we left because of what Pili had said to me two nights before. Pili was Patas's girlfriend. Standing at a hulky six feet four to Manuel's lithe five-eleven frame,

Patas was Manuel's favorite childhood playmate, who had sprouted into a giant with legs that seemed to go on forever. Thus the nickname Patas. (It would be years until I learned that his given name was actually Miguel.) I hoped that I'd like Pili because we'd obviously be spending a lot of time together as "the girlfriends." Even though my year in Salamanca seemed to prove that Spanish girls had no interest in befriending us Americans, I figured I could do my best to tone down my foreignness and make it an enjoyable evening. Pili, it seemed, had other plans.

Pili and Patas came to pick Manuel and me up for an evening out on the town in Barbate. Knowing that Spanish nightlife was always smoky, sweaty, and carried the very real potential of stepping in other people's bodily fluids, I decided to shower when the night was over, not before. But I was wearing clean clothes, and my hair looked nice. Somehow, though, my lack of showering entered our conversation, and Pili looked me up and down and uttered a word I'd never heard before, but the way she said it sounded like mud slung in my eye.

"*Guarra*," she spat.

"I'm sorry, what does that mean?" I asked.

Manuel and Patas looked embarrassed.

Waving her cigarette smoke out of her face and into mine, Pili said, "It means that's gross that you didn't shower first."

I admit I was a little taken aback. First of all, because I had always assumed that Americans were universally regarded as water wasters for showering all the time. And second, I don't think in any country it is acceptable to call someone gross after just meeting them. Later that night I confirmed it with Manuel, who admitted that even he was offended by her choice of words.

"Basically she called you a pig," Manuel said.

"And you didn't punch her in the gut for me!" I wailed.

"Sorry, you're right, I should have. But then Patas would have had to beat me up and I'd have no chance with this scrawny little body. And you'd miss me so much," he said, smiling.

I couldn't help but laugh. But secretly I wondered if Pili called me *guarra* because I was Black. I didn't want to ask Manuel because I think he already thought I was paranoid about the whole Black thing. Also, I didn't really want to know the truth. I didn't want to know for sure that Pili basically just called me a dirty nigger. Better just to speculate and call her a bunch of names in my head.

And in the meantime, just in case, for my farewell dinner, not only did I take an extra shower, I washed my hair. Nobody could call me *guarra* now.

The farewell dinner was at a restaurant called Mayte. Manuel liked to tell me that if you wanted good food in Spain, you'd never find it in a restaurant. It had to be homemade. In Salamanca that wasn't true. The food I'd eaten in most people's houses had been just as bad as the food in the restaurants. It pains me to say it, but my favorite restaurant in Sally was Burger King! After eating in the Malia home for a week, however, I realized Manuel was absolutely right. Nothing I'd consumed in Salamanca compared to the simple but delicious meals his mother made. Thick *tortilla de patatas* served with breaded chicken breasts and a simple salad. Juicy pork tenderloin smothered in a creamy Roquefort cheese sauce. And the gazpacho! In the Malia house it was thick, cold, and garlicky, the perfect complement to any Spanish meal. But for fried seafood, a specialty of the region, it was okay to eat out, I was told.

So Manuel, his brothers and sister, mom, dad, and I piled into two tiny European cars and went out for dinner. The restaurant seemed almost deserted—a bad sign, I thought. Surely if the food was good, more people would be out. But I vowed to keep an open mind and an open mouth. After all, I'd been informed that this was the family's favorite eatery, so it had to be good. Manuel's father did the ordering. His mother kept consulting with me to make sure I ate shrimp and clams and some other sea creatures with names for which I couldn't figure out the exact translation. But I said yes anyway. I knew how important food was in this culture, and I certainly didn't want them to hate me because I was a finicky eater. I still felt bad about those damn pine nuts. I vowed to eat everything that was put in front of me. When the giant shrimp with the black beady eyes staring right up at me were placed on my plate, I followed everyone else's lead, popped off the head, peeled off the shell, and ate the deliciously sweet meat. I admit, I refused to suck the juice out of the head, but that just made everyone laugh and call me "silly American." I didn't mind. Thanks to my healthy appetite, I could keep up with the Malia boys at the table, and that further cemented my place in the family. I oohed and ahhed over everything I put into my mouth and asked a lot of questions about the local cuisine, something every Spaniard is proud of. I had to bite my tongue and just nod in agreement when they unanimously criticized the food in the United States as being substandard and bad. They all cluck-clucked and felt sorry for me. I let them. Seeing as how not one of them, except Manuel, had ever been to the States and thus had no basis for an opinion, I simply chalked it up to that annoying Spanish habit of believing all things Spanish reign supreme. It was a real personal struggle, though, to keep from blurting out all of the disgusting and unhealthy foods I'd been forced to ingest in their country, like grilled pig ear sandwiches and toast slathered with flavored pig lard.

My promise to eat everything placed in front of me was sorely tested when the final plate of *raciones* made it to the table. *"¿Qué es?"* I asked as I eyed the little balls of fried green something. Manuel told me the name of the dish, which did very little to explain what they actually were. I tried to catch Manuel's eye to plead with him to give me some kind of warning if this was something I might need to hide in my napkin, but he was oblivious to my distress, as he was too busy popping the mystery balls into his mouth. Everyone was staring at me, so I poked one with my fork and placed it in my mouth, praying I'd be able to swallow it without making a face. Wouldn't you know, it was delicious. It tasted like nothing I'd ever had before, but something like a cross between a hush puppy and fried eggplant. But with a hint of the ocean.

"I know what the word for this is," Manuel said then, taking a break from stuffing his mouth.

"What?" I said, eating another one of the little balls.

"It's seaweed," he said. "Fried seaweed."

"Es muy rica," I said, smiling at my hosts. And I meant it. Fried

seaweed balls were really good. I could tell I had passed another test. I think I was winning these folks over. Bring on more deep-fried plant life; I'll eat it all, I thought, as long as it makes Manuel's family love me.

There was only one seaweed ball left.

"*Toma,*" Manuel said, offering it to me. And I ate it happily. Then I noticed Manuel's mother staring at me and then back at her son with a strange look on her face.

"What's the matter?" I asked, getting worried.

"*No es nada,*" she said. "It's just that I've never ever seen Manuel give up the last piece of food to anyone. He must really like you," she said, laughing.

"*Claro que sí,*" Manuel said, leaning over to kiss me on the cheek.

And then I knew my work was done.

⚘ I 3: Love. Life.

We spent the whole day together. For the third time in one week. We'd walked all over Brooklyn's Prospect Park, which I pointed out was so beautiful because it was designed by Frederick Law Olmsted, the same man who designed Smith College and of course that other popular green space in the city, Central Park. We were laughing and talking nonstop about movies and books and politics and our child-hoods. The only time we spent apart was when I went home to change so we could go out to dinner. I barely spoke to my two roommates as I flew in and out of the apartment, leaving them to wonder about my intentions. I was avoiding them on purpose, because if I stopped to answer the obvious question, I'd have to confront my own devious heart.

I met Michael in a Laundromat in the winter of 1995. I'd been living in New York for almost a year. Manuel had come to visit once earlier in the fall, and we'd had a wonderful time together, but he still had a year of school left in Spain and then who knew what the future held. We still loved each other, but we were both too practical to hold on to something so uncertain. "If you meet a wonderful Spanish girl back in Salamanca," I had told him tearfully when he left my cozy Brooklyn apartment, "please fall in love with her so we can end this crazy romance." He of-fered me the same get-out-of-jail-free card. He being the fatalist and I the optimist, we both agreed that if it was meant to be, then it would be. But we were too young, too poor, and too far apart to nurture this like a real relationship. And that's what I repeated to myself as I splashed on my Calyx perfume and applied my signature burgundy-wine-colored lipstick as I got ready to go out with Michael again.

Michael had just graduated from the New School with a master of fine arts in creative writing. He was originally from Indianapolis and was determined to get his novel sold to a major publisher. Even though he stood well over six feet tall and had the physical build of a linebacker, he had a teddy bear persona and was quick to inject humor and sarcasm into any conversation. We had a lot in common as wannabe writers from the Midwest living only blocks apart in Park Slope, Brooklyn. And best of all, he was Black. Like me. Unlike my conversations with Manuel, Michael and I could talk forever about our favorite episodes of *What's Happening!!* and *Fat Albert*, shows that never made it over to Spain. We could reminisce about being the only Black child many times growing up in our corn-fed midwestern lives. He teased me mercilessly about my lack of experience with "our kind of people," but I didn't mind. And I managed to talk all about my year living in Spain, my shattered dreams about living abroad, and not once mention Manuel. Technically we weren't a couple, so why bring it up? I told myself. There were no rings on my fingers, I reasoned, and I was only going to live once. Besides, wouldn't a normal relationship with a nice Black man be better for me anyway? I'd have a date to accompany me to all these silly office parties I had to go to now that I worked for a big-time corporate public relations agency in Manhattan. We could talk on the phone without my taking out a personal loan to pay for the charges. And best of all, walking down the street with Michael, I wouldn't call attention to myself as I did with Manuel, where even homeless women sometimes took offense at our interracial romance.

"Do you want to go out for Thai?" Michael asked me when I got back to his house. I said sure even though I hadn't completely gotten over the posttraumatic stress disorder related to my experience as a Thai waitress.

We walked to the restaurant, taking our time to window-shop at all the cute stores and boutiques down Park Slope's bustling Seventh Avenue. Park Slope felt like an amped-up Northampton to me, complete with happy lesbians, a diverse crowd, and plenty of ethnic restaurants. I often ran into other Smithies when I walked around, amazed at how all of us ended up in the same New York neighborhood. Sometimes

I laughed when I remembered how scared I was initially to move to New York, especially Brooklyn. I was so sure I'd have to live locked behind bars with seven roommates subsisting on ramen noodles and Kool-Aid. Instead, I lived in a beautiful brownstone apartment with two other girls, paying only $450 a month. We lived a block from Prospect Park, an inch from the subway, and one block from the action on Seventh Avenue. I loved my life (except for the fact that I was working in PR, sending out press releases for candy bars and powdered soup instead of writing the next great American novel). And here I was with almost a new boyfriend. I smiled at the thought.

"What are you laughing at?" Michael asked me, noticing my smile. We were seated at Rice Thai restaurant, close to the window so we could watch the people walking along the avenue.

"Nothing," I said, not wanting to admit that I had been fantasizing about the two of us as a couple.

We ate our dinner, with our usual nonstop conversation about writing and making it in New York. I admired the way Michael spoke with conviction about his success. He described himself as a novelist, not an "aspiring" this or "wannabe" that. He spoke of "whens," not "ifs," when it came to his success. His future was clear in his mind, unlike me, who spent at least one hour every night scribbling furiously in my journal wondering if I had what it took to be a real writer.

Once I swallowed the last noodle from the plate of pad Thai and slurped down the last milky sweet dregs of my Thai iced tea, Michael put on his serious face and shifted the conversation. "Can we talk about us?" he started.

Suddenly my hands went cold and I started to feel nervous.

"What about us?" I asked stupidly.

"Well, I like you, and I'd like us to be more than friends," he said plainly.

I squirmed in my seat, trying to figure out how to respond. Five minutes ago I was imagining what our children would look like and now that the offer was on the table I felt so conflicted. My mind immediately flashed back to Manuel. I still loved him and didn't think it was fair or possible to love one but be with another. I wished Michael hadn't spoken the words aloud, because then I could just hover in this undefined state that wouldn't require me to *decide* anything. We could just be. I could reap the benefits of having male attention without officially betraying Manuel. God, I hated this.

"Well, I kind of have sort of like a boyfriend," I stuttered, despising myself for having gone this long without mentioning Manuel. Now I sounded like I was hiding him, which I guess I was, but not with bad intentions.

"You do?" Michael said, not bothering to hide his surprise and what looked like hurt behind his golden-brown eyes.

I quickly scrambled to explain. "Well, he's not like a regular boyfriend. I mean he's in Spain and we're not technically together because he's there and I'm here but . . ."

"But what?" Michael pressed.

I couldn't go on, because what I was about to say was "If I met someone I liked better than Manuel then I'd forget all about him, but sorry, Michael, that's not going to be you." And like that I realized that even though I really, really liked Michael, I didn't like him more than Manuel. And I swore I wouldn't give up on Manuel unless something so much better came along. But really, what guy wants to hear that? So instead I said, "But he's going to come to the States when he finishes school in a year and I promised I'd wait for him until then."

"So were you going to tell me about *el señor*, or what?" Michael asked. And I couldn't tell if he was angry or teasing me again.

"I was going to tell you," I said, but I didn't know if I would have or not. I quickly ran through all of my interactions with Michael then, our days and nights spent together to make sure I hadn't crossed the official friend line and I couldn't be branded a tease, even though I knew I had been. I admit it. I just hoped Michael wouldn't throw his water in my face, storm out of the restaurant, and call me a dick tease. Or worse, cry.

Of course he didn't. He just kind of shook his head at my behavior and commenced a relentless barrage of questions and merciless teasing about why I liked a probably effeminate Spaniard over his hulking example of manhood. I took it all, thankful it hadn't turned ugly. And stopping only for a moment to wonder why Michael hadn't fought a little harder for my affections.

◊   ◊   ◊   ◊

We were discussing marriage. Literally, trying to decide if we should get married or go our separate ways. At least that's the way I saw it. It was 1998 and Manuel and I had been an on-again, off-again, long-distance, in-love, in-hate couple for six years. We'd been through more of my "shouldn't I be with my own kind" crushes on other Black men and one woman. He'd been called back to Spain, once by his guilty conscience for abandoning the family business, and once by the Spanish army demanding he come fulfill his military obligation. We'd broken up at least three times and consulted an astrologer on a couple of occasions. But now I was twenty-seven years old and realized that if this "affair to remember" wasn't heading toward "endless love," I had to move on.

"So basically you're giving me an ultimatum," Manuel summed up, his English nearly flawless after his having lived in New York City for three years.

"No," I said, trying to clarify. "I'm just saying if we're not going to get married, I think I need to walk away from you, because what's the point?"

"Well, that's not fair," Manuel protested.

"Why not?" I asked, not sensing any injustice in the option I'd laid out.

"Well, I don't want to break up with you," Manuel said, "but I'm not sure about marriage."

Putting on my best therapist voice, copied from my mother, I asked, "Well, what do *you* want, Manuel?"

"Well," he began thoughtfully, "I want us to take the next step. I want to live with you and set up a house with you and buy furniture and cook together and not have to worry about other people," he said. I knew he was referring to my best friend and roommate, Gael. She and I were so close, our own parents couldn't tell us apart on the telephone.

"You know what?" I countered. "That to me sounds a lot like marriage. In fact, that sounds exactly like marriage. Especially since I have no plans on living with any guy without being married first."

"Are you serious?" he said.

"As a heart attack," I said.

"Why not?" Manuel asked, as if I had just admitted I was never going to shower again.

"Because there's no point. Living with someone takes so much work and compromise. I'm not willing to go there unless it's for happily ever after," I said, meaning every word. I wasn't about to pick up somebody else's dirty socks or admit my shit really does stink, with no guarantee at the other end.

"But what if I don't want to get married?" Manuel pressed. He had a master plan for his life, which didn't involve walking down any aisles until he was at least thirty-five. It was an arbitrary number, but it meant something to him nonetheless.

"You don't have to," I said, meaning it. I wasn't jonesing for a proposal, just some clarity about our future. At that point I felt like I could marry this man and be perfectly happy or, being the resilient type, walk away (with plenty of days spent crying and eating chocolate, of course) and start over with someone new. Not Michael, though, because he'd met a wonderful woman and married her less than a year later and then relocated to Miami, where he swore he'd be inspired to write a better novel.

Manuel paused to mull this all over.

"So let me get this straight," he finally said. "If we're not getting married, it's over."

"Yeah, I guess so," I said, not liking the way that sounded so final, but realizing it had come to that. It did sound like an ultimatum, and basically it was, but I wasn't setting it up for my gain. I thought it was in both of our best interests. Neither one of us had ever had a serious relationship with anyone else and if we weren't going to make this one forever, then we should get out there and find someone new. Maybe Manuel would like to try being with a girl who wasn't so bossy and demanding. Maybe I'd like to find a guy with oodles of money who could shower me with expensive gifts and fly me all over the world. Manuel interrupted my musing.

"Okay, let's get married then," he said.

"Are you serious?" I said, sitting up on the bed, where I had been sprawled out for this discussion. Suddenly this felt serious.

"Well, yeah. I don't want to lose you," Manuel said. "And really the next step is for us to live together and set up a house together. For you that means marriage. I'd be fine just living together, but I also don't really care."

"So does that mean we're getting married?" I asked, suddenly feeling like a lottery winner who had just realized she hit all three numbers. Maybe I did care more than I let on.

Manuel smiled at me then and teased, "Do you want to?"

I smiled back. "Yeah. I guess so." And just like that, I realized we weren't just theorizing. And suddenly I wasn't so clearheaded. I was seized with panic.

"Wait, are we ready for this?"

Now it was Manuel's turn to reassure me. "You just said so yourself. This is the next logical step for us. We both want to go there. You want to get married. So let's do it. I want to make a home with you, Titi," he said. And I believed him.

"Ohmigod!" I screamed into my pillow. I didn't want to annoy Gael in the other room. "I'm getting married!" Surprising even myself, I jumped up and did a crazy happy dance around my bedroom, chanting, "I'm getting married. I'm getting married." Manuel soon joined me, making his happy dance even goofier than mine. We then both collapsed on the bed, laughing. Sobering up, I looked at Manuel lying next to me and said, "Can we call my parents? I think you should ask their permission."

After all these years, Manuel had a very open relationship with my mother. It had taken my father longer to warm up to this young foreigner who wanted to steal his daughter. But once they bonded over NBA basketball, my father found a kindred spirit in Manuel, even though he still had a hard time understanding his accent.

I picked up the phone and dialed my parents' number in Milwaukee. My mom answered the phone and I asked her to get Dad on. Then I handed

Manuel the phone. As I listened to the conversation, hearing my mother scream through the phone, I started to cry. Manuel and I had worked so hard to get to this point and here we were after all, making it official.

I planned my wedding from my cubicle at *Entertainment Weekly* magazine, where I was now employed as a reporter, which was a nice way of saying fact-checker. The wedding would take place in Milwaukee and yet would be festooned with elements from Spain. I wanted to make sure the celebration was a true bicultural experience with both Black and Spanish cultures equally represented. I didn't want Manuel's family or my own to feel neglected.

"Is there a Spanish wedding march?" I asked Manuel one morning as we lazed in bed in our new apartment. We had moved in together in November. The wedding was slated for April 3, to coincide with Semana Santa so all the Spaniards would be able to come, since Spain virtually shuts down for Holy Week.

"A what?" he asked me, trying to remain asleep while I peppered him with questions.

"You know, a song that gets played when the bride and groom walk down the aisle," I explained.

"I'm not sure," he said. "But I don't think so." Throughout the months of planning, it had become abundantly clear that Manuel knew very little about Spanish wedding customs. So I'd been relying on the Internet and my own creative imagination. For example, I'd decided to find a flamenco guitarist to play as our guests came into the sanctuary. And as luck would have it, the one flamenco guitarist in Milwaukee, who was not Spanish, knew the one flamenco singer in Milwaukee who was Spanish *and* she came from a small town in the south of Spain not far from Manuel's home. What are the odds? I wondered, as I called her to see if she'd be available to sing at our wedding. Of course I didn't know if flamenco music was appropriate for a wedding, but it made sense to me. And for the Black music portion, I asked a cousin of mine to sing one of my favorite gospel hymns. When she heard my request, she politely declined, explaining that my selection was more appropriate for funerals, but she'd come up with another option she was sure I'd like. And I did because I wasn't very hard to please when it came to this wedding. I just wanted everyone to have a good time and feel the energy of these two cultures coming together.

We chose to have the ceremony in a Unitarian church close to my parents' home. By that time, I was a member of the Baha'i faith, which doesn't have any prescribed wedding rituals, and Manuel was a deeply lapsed Catholic. We figured a Unitarian church was liberal enough to house our combined religious backgrounds. The reception was going to be at a random country club not far from the church. I chose a meal that reflected Manuel's and my shared delight in eating, starting with a seafood bisque followed by a Spanish chicken stew and spring vegetable risotto. The wedding cake was a four-tiered strawberry shortcake, and I had secretly arranged to get a groom's cake for Manuel made out of strawberry ice cream. That was his only request. "Can we get a wedding cake made out of ice cream?" I laughed when he asked me, besotted as he was by the concept of an ice cream cake. I couldn't wait for him to see it.

"Well, what song do you want to hear when I come floating down the aisle?" I pressed Manuel again. He wasn't biting, preferring to burrow deeper into his pillow.

I loved these lazy mornings in bed and wanted to get a conversation going, so I changed topics.

"You know what I just realized?" I started. "Our kids will basically be Cuban." That got Manuel's attention.

"What?" he said, sitting up to look at me with an eyebrow raised.

"Yeah, they'll be half Black and half Spanish. Essentially, isn't that what a Cuban is? Or a Puerto Rican, for that matter, or someone from the Dominican Republic?"

"Actually," Manuel corrected me, "our kids will be half Black and half Spanish. You can't just give birth to a Cuban."

"I know," I said. "But still, they'll probably look Cuban or Puerto Rican or something."

"As long as they have your perky nose and beautiful skin, I don't care what they look like," Manuel said, pulling me close to cuddle. I melted into his embrace and we clasped hands and held them above our heads, admiring how nicely they fit together. Sometimes it hit us at the exact same time how incredible it was that we had found each other in a German class in Salamanca: a Black American and a Spaniard from a small fishing village. And we were still in love and getting married and living in one of the most exciting cities in the world.

When we considered all of the bizarre coincidences of our coupling, it almost made us believe that some higher calling had brought us together. Like his childhood threat of marrying a Black woman and his obsession with the English language. And likewise my profound belief that Spain would play an important role in my life. Not to mention the fact that his sister and my sister both had the same name, Elisa. Spelled the same way. And that Manuel and my father shared the same birthday. When you added up all these karmic circumstances, I firmly believed I was meant to be with this man. These random connections sustained me when I had doubts that this relationship wouldn't be able to weather our cultural differences.

I rolled over on my side to face Manuel then to ask a more serious question. "If our kids look Latino, will they have a hard time in Spain? Because your people are truly racist when it comes to South Americans," I said. And then I added, "Or worse, they'll look Moroccan." I knew the Moroccans who stole across the Straits of Gibraltar looking for work were not well regarded by the Spanish populace.

Manuel made light of my worries. "Our kids will just look Spanish. People won't assume they're Puerto Rican or Moroccan or anything," he said, just a tad bit defensively, I thought.

"Manuel, they're going to be brown. People are going to assume they are something other than Spanish, because—news flash— Spaniards aren't brown."

"What do you know?" Manuel challenged. "I happen to have friends who we call '*negro*' because they get as dark as you in the summer. And their hair is really curly," he added, knowing my obsession with hair as the true marker of a person's ethnic origins.

"But they're not permanently Black or brown. They're just suntanned and that's not the same thing. And please tell me you know that, just as you know that if our future children look Moroccan or South American they are going to have problems."

"I don't *know* about that," Manuel said, unwilling to contemplate his future offspring being shunned in his own country. He altered the arc of the conversation. "Whatever they look like, if they get your skin and my long bones they are going to be so beautiful." And like that he got me off course. All he had to do was start speculating about our beautiful children and I was a goner, so happy to succumb to beautiful mixed-race fantasies. Living in Park Slope, Brooklyn, where every other family on the street seemed to be a member of the rainbow coalition, with one child more beautiful than the next, it was easy to get caught up in the rapture. I admit it. I couldn't wait to procreate with Manuel.

"I just had a brilliant idea," I said, sitting up in bed.

"What?" Manuel asked, pulling me back to nestle beside him.

"If we started a family business, I know what it should be called," I said.

"What kind of family business?" Manuel asked.

"I'm not sure yet," I answered, giddy with my new idea. "But you know, something that speaks to our Black Spanish, or Blanish, cultures. Okay, basically I've just come up with our family expression."

"Our what?" Manuel asked.

"Like if we had a family logo or brand. I know what it would be."

"What?"

"Brace yourself," I said, pausing for dramatic effect. "Kinky Gazpacho! Is that perfect or what?"

Manuel smiled. "I do like it. 'Cause I'm feeling very kinky right now."

I swatted his roving hand away, jazzed up on this idea. "No, really, I mean, how perfect! Maybe it should be the title of a book about the story of our lives or something. We do have a good story," I said. "We could write it together."

"How about you write it and I'll translate it into Spanish," Manuel offered.

"Fine," I said, loving the way the words sounded so perfectly incongruous together, like the way Manuel and I looked when we strolled down the street hand in hand.

"Kinky Gazpacho."

14: How Do You Say "Aunt Jemima" in Spanish?

Right before I left for Spain in the summer of 1999, my first time back as a married woman, I read an essay about the dangers of traveling with dreadlocks. How they are often perceived as a symbol of the drug trade and in some countries are even considered illegal. I paid close attention to the story because I was now sporting dreadlocks that hung nicely down my back in long, thick ropes. Luckily the essay hadn't mentioned anything about Spain being a dreadlock danger zone, but still I kept my guard up. And that's why I immediately copped an attitude when an undercover police officer accosted me in the airport in Madrid telling me I was suspected of transporting illegal drugs.

"Do you speak English?" the man dressed in a shiny polyester suit and sunglasses asked me while we were walking from the terminal to the new airport train that would shuttle us into downtown Madrid.

Since Manuel was now making a living as a high school teacher with his summers free, he'd left for Spain a month before me. I had only two weeks of vacation, so I was meeting him there, accompanied by my brother, Lee. It pained me to say it, but after a three-week sojourn in Costa Rica during high school and one year of college-level Spanish, Lee's accent was better than mine. And despite his mere nineteen years, he was strong and burly and made a comforting traveling companion.

I took in the man's tacky yellow suit and outdoor glasses worn inside and wondered why I didn't guess when I noticed him earlier that he was an undercover police officer. Typical in a 1980s *Miami Vice* kind of way. I told him that I did indeed speak English but didn't bother to answer his questions. Lee and I just kept walking, intent on making our train to the city.

"Well," he said, staying close to me, "we were expecting a large shipment of illegal drugs on your airplane and we'd like to check your bags and identification." And then he added, trying to make me feel better about being singled out, "It's not just you, we're checking many people from that flight."

Even though in my previous life I'd always abhorred loud Black people who feel it is their duty and their right to make public spectacles of themselves when they think the Man has done them wrong, I felt my inner Angry Black Woman get ready to roar.

Still without breaking my stride, I said, rather loudly, "Look, you're just targeting me because I'm Black. I don't have any drugs in my suitcase and I'm rushing for my train, so you'll just have to search someone else." I paused for a moment and looked around me to see if I had caused a stir. To see if anyone would indeed become incensed by this obviously racist act committed by an agent of the law. But nothing happened. People just kept moving on their way and I felt the first niggles of fear that the police might actually detain me.

"It will only take a short while," the officer pressed. "I just need to see your passport and examine your luggage. We can go right this way," he said, gesturing to what looked like an exit to the airport parking lot.

Just as I was about to suggest that if he wanted to examine anything of mine that he do it out in the open so the Spanish public could witness the injustice perpetuated by their very own law enforcement agents, my brother leaned over to whisper in my ear, "Why don't you ask to see his ID first?"

As soon as he said that, my bullshit detector came out of hibernation. "Good point," I whispered to Lee. "Can I see some ID?" I asked the guy as we came to a place where we'd either go left and hit the escalator to the train or go right into the parking lot. Before we could make the decision, he took off running in the opposite direction like all of sudden the hounds of hell were nipping at his heels. And just like that, they were. Out of nowhere, what seemed like a gazillion members of Spain's *guardia civil* materialized out of the woodwork and started chasing the guy in the tacky suit. And just as quickly, Lee and I were surrounded by real police officers, in real uniforms, with real guns.

One of them approached us and spoke in Spanish.

"Are you with that man?" he asked.

"That guy who just ran away?" I responded. "No way. He said he was a police officer and suggested I might be carrying drugs." As soon as I said that I wished I hadn't. Why bring up the drug thing in front of the real police? Fear and a foreign language can make you say really stupid things.

"Are you certain you do not know him?" the officer pressed

I started to panic then, thinking perhaps my Black skin and dreadlocks would land me in a Spanish prison after all. My jet-lagged brain could barely process what was happening, but my little brother, whom I've always taken care of, was standing beside me waiting to see how I was going to handle this. Now was not the time to get hysterical and fall apart.

"Honestly," I began, hoping that the nervousness in my voice wasn't misconstrued as guilt. "We were just walking to catch the train and he started following us, asking to see our passports and luggage. I thought he was a policeman."

The officer seemed to be considering my story and then held up his hand to signal that we should stay put while he went to consult with his colleagues. I wanted to mention that we were trying to make a train, but I didn't really think these guys cared.

Lee and I tried to tell what was happening, but we didn't know how to read Spanish body language and we couldn't make out what they were whispering to one another. While we waited, we did manage to buy a train ticket at the kiosk behind us. Then the officer who told us to wait came back over to where we were standing.

"Come with me," he said. This time we followed without hesitating. We took the escalator down to the train platform, where we practically tripped over the shiny-suited con man who was now lying facedown on the floor with an officer strapping on handcuffs. We must have just missed a train because there was nobody else down there waiting.

"Please sit," the officer said to us. We sat on a bench and then answered what seemed to be the same three questions about one hundred times.

"Why are you in Spain?"

"Where are you going?"

"Where are you staying?"

Even though I said over and over again that I did not know the man who was now looking very unhappy a short distance away, and even though the police officer claimed he believed me, I still felt guilty of some crime. Suddenly I wished my slim wedding ring was bigger and bolder. Finally, the officer and his female partner seemed satisfied with our story of visiting my new in-laws in Andalucía. They allowed us to board the next train and gave us an escort to ensure we made it to the main train station without incident. Or maybe it was to make sure we left their city without causing further harm. Regardless, as soon as the doors closed and we pulled away from the airport, I couldn't hold it in any longer. I burst into tears, vowing I'd never travel without my Spanish husband in Spain again. I was an easy target for con men and police alike. That was me, a big Black moving target . . . with dreadlocks.

Despite my brush with the law, I didn't give up on Spain. Even though I was sorely tempted after a visit to the south of France, where I stayed with my host sister Salwa from Morocco. She had married a wealthy Frenchman and lived in a picturesque French château with olive and almond trees dotting her backyard. It felt like heaven to me. Instantly. For some reason I felt an immediate affinity for France and wondered why Spain never felt like that to me. I wanted to love Spain wholeheartedly and without reservation. I wanted so badly to feel connected to the land and its people. I wanted to let my guard down and feel at peace when I stepped on Spanish soil, but so far that peace was escaping me.

I tried to bring up the discussion with Manuel, but he always took my praise of another country as a criticism of his own. Which truth be told, it was. It didn't help that it seemed that every one of my friends, Black, White, and Other, after returning from trips to Spain couldn't help but gush to my husband about how much they luuuuvved his country. The food. The friendly people. The laid-back culture. Me? All I could do was complain about the absence of Black people and the lack of any sort of cultural awareness.

In the years since moving to New York, I'd finally experienced my own Black Is Beautiful awakening. A series of events, including working at *Vibe* magazine, writing a book about the cultural history of Black hair in America, and just living in the vibrant Black community of Fort Greene, Brooklyn, made me finally so very proud of my Black skin. Of my heritage. Of my people. Of my hair. I didn't want to hide anymore, and I didn't want to apologize for who I was. I had gone from being the Undercover Sister to the Angry Black Woman to just being comfortable in my own skin. I no longer feared speaking up about race and injustice in a crowd of non-Black people. I enjoyed the company of my own kind. I was living my revolution, so I had no interest in a country that didn't celebrate diversity. I no longer needed Spain to be a place for me to escape to; I needed it to be a place that welcomed all of me with open arms.

After the summer of the big fake drug bust, Manuel and I returned to Spain in time for Carnaval. Manuel had often spoken of his love for the weeklong festival where costumed people would party in the streets all night long. There would be parades and pageants and a basic feeling of revelry before the austerity of Lent and Semana Santa. Basically, it was like Mardi Gras in Spain.

"But it's not," Manuel continued to stress. "Carnaval in the south of Spain is different than anywhere else in the world," he said.

"Why? How is different?" I asked.

"In the south, we use the parades and the performances to complain about the government or to make fun of a certain politician or something. It's very political. But we're funny about it. I crack up listening to these guys. They're hilarious," Manuel said.

I knew Manuel was excited for me to see Carnaval in Cádiz, but nighttime reveling with free-flowing alcohol and people wearing masks? Sounded like a recipe for disaster and a good time to hide under the bed. But of course I couldn't do that. I tried to keep my mind open and prepared myself to be enlightened by men in drag.

"Hello, my sister," a woman, possibly drunk, said to me in heavily accented English as Manuel and I muscled our way into a crowded club. I looked at the girl in her Wilma Flintstone caveman dress, the fake bone in her nose, and her skin stained black with what appeared to be black shoe polish and wanted to punch her in the face. Since being out at Carnaval, I had seen dozens of Spaniards—men and women— decked out in Aunt Jemima gear. Colorful head rags, matching skirts, and oversize tits and asses. The costume was completed with that black shoe polish smeared all over their skin.

"What are they supposed to be?" I demanded from Manuel, trying to decide if I should be outraged or scared. Were these people making fun of Black women because they found us cute like bunny rabbits and wanted to see what it would feel like to be us, or did they find us repulsive and by dressing up like an exaggerated mammy seek to show their dislike? Either way I didn't feel comfortable in the streets of Cádiz that night. So by the time my boneheaded sister sought me out in a "sisterly" embrace, I'd had enough.

"Don't call me sister," I practically spat at this drunken reveler. "Do I look like you?" I demanded. The girl looked stricken and didn't say anything. So I said it again, louder.

"Do I look like you? Do I have a bone in my nose? Does my skin look like tar? I am not your sister." My rage threatened to erupt into violence. I clenched my fingers together in a fist and got ready to punch her. I wanted to rip the bone right out of her nose. Manuel sensed I was near the edge and quickly steered me away from the girl and out of the club. Once we got outside I took some deep breaths and tried to calm down. Gain some perspective. Manuel took my hand, wisely not saying anything, and led me toward an outdoor *churros y chocolate* stand. If there's anything in Spain that can always cheer me up, it's fried sticks of dough rolled in sugar and dipped in thick, rich chocolate.

Having lived in New York City for five years, and away from Carnaval for just as long, even Manuel saw this practice of dressing up "Black" as a disturbing phenomenon. But he sheepishly admitted that it had always been one of the favorite and easiest costumes for Carnaval. I didn't want to discuss it on the street, but I knew we'd get back to the conversation. In the meantime, I wanted to find something besides *churros y chocolate* that was pleasant about Carnaval. So we followed the sound of live music and came across a band playing on a stage in one of the city's plazas. I didn't know if I should laugh or cry as we pushed our way toward the front of the stage and saw that the members of the all-male band were dressed as bodacious black mammies, with color-coordinated polka-dot skirts. It was enough to make me laugh at the absurdity. "Why?" I screamed at the top of my lungs, trying to be heard over the music, but to no avail. I totally felt like Laurence Fishburne at the end of Spike Lee's movie *School Daze*.

"Let's go home," Manuel said.

"This is why I could never live in your country," I said in response, wondering if people were looking at me and comparing me to the fools singing on the stage. Now I feared that maybe Spaniards did look at me and see only a stereotype.

Manuel just grunted, probably afraid of what I might say.

All I could say was an expression my maternal grandfather, Papa Willie, used regularly when dealing with the knuckleheads in this world. "Ain't that some shit!"

◊   ◊   ◊   ◊

Our first child was born on June 10, 2001, in New York City. Manuel and I agreed that if it was a boy we would give him a Spanish name. After debating until the day he came home from the hospital, we settled on Esai Manuel. It was Spanish in origin, but not from Spain per se, which Manuel's family immediately pointed out, somewhat miffed that we had not followed the family tradition of naming the child after the father. In Manuel's family, therefore, only three or four names were repeatedly recycled. So now not only had Manuel defected to America and married an American—a Black American at that—he 'd picked some crazy South American–sounding name for his firstborn son. I suspected I wasn't winning any popularity contests with the Malia family.

My paranoia about the Spanish people accepting my son was rearing its ugly head once Esai was a real being and not just a theoretical issue confronting Manuel and me. Even though Esai was so pale that people constantly asked me if I was his nanny, I still worried whether Manuel's family would accept him or not. Especially with his kooky name. And I worried that when he got older, kids in Spain might chase him in the streets, chanting hot cocoa commercial lyrics. Cola Cao, after all, was still a popular drink, and the Black ladies still graced the box. Manuel listened to my concerns and repeatedly tried to calm my fears.

"My people are ignorant, yes," he'd say. "But we're not racist. And Esai will be fine. People won't even know he's not Spanish."

I tried to believe him. I wanted to believe him. I wanted Spain to revert to my childhood fantasy. I wanted Esai to benefit from being of two distinct cultures. But stuff just kept happening that didn't allow me to loosen my grip on my Negro paranoia.

For example, somebody gave me a CD of Mediterranean lullabies as a gift. The songs were in different languages and native speakers sang each one. The song titled "Duerme negrito" caught my attention right away. From the title I knew it was in Spanish and that it was about a little Black child. I got excited since Manuel had selective amnesia and couldn't remember a single lullaby in his native language. Finally, I'd have something to sing to our child in Spanish, I thought. Already obsessed that his bilingualism would be delayed if he didn't hear Spanish lullabies, I paid close attention to the words so I could memorize them. But the more I listened, the more I doubted my linguistic abilities. I had to be understanding something wrong. The lyrics I heard, loosely translated, went like this:

Sleep, sleep, little black boy, your mama's in the fields.
Sleep, sleep, little boy. She's going to bring quail for you,

She's going to bring fresh fruit for you, she's going to bring pork for
    you,
She's going to bring many things for you.
And if the little black boy doesn't go to sleep,
The white devil will come and—zap!—he'll eat your little foot!
Sleep, sleep, little black boy, your mama's in the fields, little boy.
She's working hard, working, yes, and they don't pay her.
Working, and she's coughing; working, yes, for her sweet little black
    boy.

I swear, if that's not an exact translation, it's pretty close. I played
the song for Manuel, incensed and wondering if he'd ever heard this
horrible "lullaby" before. As soon as the first strains of the song came
on, Manuel threw his head back, closed his eyes, and started singing
along. Before he could stop himself, he yelled out in glee, "I know this
song. I remember it from when I was little."

"What!" I said. "You know this song? It's horrible." Manuel had the
good sense then to look a little embarrassed.

"You know, I never really thought about it." Thankfully he took the
time then to do so. After listening for a moment, he turned to me and
started to chuckle. "I can't believe how horrible that is," he said. "I
never noticed before."

"How could you not notice?" I asked. "Did your mother sing you
this song? You never asked about the white devil biting the little black
boy's foot off?"

Manuel knew he really shouldn't even attempt to answer me when
I was in this state.

"What if she sings this to Esai?" I wailed. "He'll be fucked up for
life. Do you see what I mean? Your people and your country just have
no freaking idea about my people. And I'm sorry, this song is racist."
I picked up the CD case and looked at the song credits. Indeed, it
said the song "Negrito" came from Spain. Manuel couldn't even claim
that they had co-opted the song from the Americas. Nope, a nonracist
Spaniard wrote the song. I knew my postpregnancy hormones were
still in full effect, but I didn't think I was overreacting. I later learned

that even though this song was one of Manuel's childhood favorites, it did not come from Spain. It is thought to be Cuban in origin, and then it spread to the rest of the Spanish-speaking world and eventually to my living room in Brooklyn.

We took Esai on his first trip to Spain in November, when he was five months old. Manuel wanted to make sure his grandmother got a chance to meet her first great-grandchild before it was too late. His grandfather, the one who'd told me the racist joke at our first meeting, had already died. His wife, la Abuela Inés, now lived with Manuel's parents in their new house in the "suburbs." In anticipation of Esai's birth, Ines had reinvigorated her arthritic hands to knit our baby the most delicate sweaters and matching booties and a fancy woolen coat and hat for a christening that would never happen. I had to thank her in person. As expected, Cha-Cha, as Manuel called his *abuela*, wept when she saw Esai, having been convinced she wouldn't live to see the day. The entire family showered Esai with gifts, fought over who would hold him, and took oodles of pictures. They could not exclaim enough over his beauty, seemingly proud of his multiracial features. I was pleasantly surprised. He was shown off to the neighbors and colleagues at work. Safely nestled in the cocoon of Manuel's family's adoration and appreciation for our child, I felt a real part of the family. It felt old-fashioned, but having Esai, I felt like perhaps I had bridged a gap. Even if Manuel's family and the rest of Spain still didn't really understand the Black experience, they now had this biracial ambassador in whom they could see themselves more clearly.

We had only ten days to spend in Spain, since Manuel had had to make a special request for the time off from work. I was still on maternity leave from *Entertainment Weekly*. Two days before we were due to fly back home, Manuel informed me that we had to go visit his paternal grandmother because she wanted to meet Esai, too. This was huge. In all my years of coming to Spain, I had never met this woman. Manuel's father had issued a cryptic warning early on in our relationship that his mother might say something rude (translation: racist) to me, so there was no reason to introduce us. I didn't think this was too odd since Manuel had informed me that relations with the paternal side of his family had always been strained. He never wanted to visit his cousins, aunts, or grandmother, preferring to maintain the status quo of pretending they didn't exist. The bad blood went way back, apparently. But who doesn't have family drama, I always reasoned, and never gave it much thought.

But now *la otra abuela* had decided that the silence had gone on long enough and we had been summoned. She wanted to see her great-grandson. Before we left for Barbate, Manuel's mother tried to prepare him. I couldn't follow the entire conversation, but I gathered the poor woman was practically an invalid so we shouldn't stay too long and overtax her. Manuel was only too happy to oblige.

Manuel didn't say much on the twenty-minute drive over. As we got closer to Barbate, I made sure Esai hadn't spit up or drooled on his clothes. I noticed that the Spaniards were way more fastidious about their baby clothes than the average American. I put Esai in Old Navy rompers for almost any outing, and my mother-in-law wanted to know why the poor child was always wearing pajamas. Manuel stopped the car. When I looked out the window to see where we were, I noticed we were in front of Manuel's old house. The one I had visited on my first trip to meet his parents.

"Why are we here?" I asked.

"Because this is where my grandmother lives," Manuel answered as if I'd asked a really dumb question.

"In your old house?" I said.

"No, the one attached to it," he clarified.

"You mean, all those times I was here, your grandmother was in the house next door and we never went to say hello?" I asked incredulously.

"Yeah, my father said not to bother. And apparently she would always watch you coming in and out of my house from the window, so she knows what you look like and everything. She just never wanted to talk to you." I pondered this information. And then Manuel said, "I told you she was special. Come on, let's get this over with."

Before Manuel could ring the buzzer, an older woman with happy, sparkly blue eyes and weather-wrinkled skin threw the door wide open.

"Pepa!" Manuel cried, opening his arms to wrap the woman in a huge hug. I knew this must be the woman who had helped raise Manuel's father, Manuel, and his three siblings and was now his grandmother's caretaker and companion. She'd been an employee of Manuel's grandmother for more than fifty years.

Pepa then turned to me, planted welcoming kisses on both my cheeks, and gently eased Esai out of my arms as if she'd been waiting for him forever. Keeping up a constant chatter, she ushered us into the salon. I was so nervous, wondering how this family matriarch would size me up. Maybe she would say something racist to me now. Maybe she would spit on me. Maybe she wouldn't want me to sit on her furniture.

My worries were in vain.

Manuel's grandmother was a frail, feeble, wrinkly old woman with her swollen feet propped up in a chair and double-thick eyeglasses covering the majority of her tiny face. When she spoke, the words came out in weak whispers, barely audible. Manuel chatted her up like the pro that he was, complimenting her on the house, asking about her health, talking about his life in the States. She kept up with the conversation, shaking her finger in his direction occasionally to make a point. She seemed perfectly harmless, so I busied myself keeping Esai happy, making sure he didn't put his pudgy fingers on anything that appeared fragile. I was glad Manuel was keeping his grandmother occupied so I didn't have to participate in the conversation. I couldn't quite understand her accent and didn't want to embarrass her by asking her to repeat herself.

Pepa left the room and soon returned to offer us tea and coffee. So we sipped and slurped with the TV providing a welcome background noise. When we were just about finished, Manuel's grandmother motioned for Pepa to go get something for her. When she came back, she passed an envelope full of money for Esai over to Manuel. It was from la Abuela, Pepa explained. I was stunned by her generosity and wondered if Manuel's father hadn't been too harsh with his assessment of his mother. Clearly she had mellowed with age and was just trying to reconnect with her family now. Better late than never, I thought. Babies really can work magic, I realized, hugging my miracle child.

When we got home, back to Manuel's parents' house, his mother was waiting for us in the kitchen.

"How did it go?" she asked us as we sat around the table munching on fresh walnuts.

"It went really well," I said, before Manuel could answer. "She was really nice. She gave us a lot of money for Esai and she just seemed really sweet," I said.

Manuel's mother seemed dubious. She raised a questioning eyebrow at Manuel as if to say "Really?"

"She was the same as she always is," Manuel announced, looking at me with a mixture of pity and regret.

"Why did you say that? She was just a pitiful old woman who could barely talk," I said.

Manuel's mother refused to look me in the eye, suddenly getting very busy pulling the meat from the shell of her walnut.

"Lori, she was ignoring you," Manuel said to me. "She refused to talk to her," he said to his mother, shaking his head in disbelief.

"I knew something like that would happen," his mother said, looking pained and apologetic.

I was almost laughing then. "I just thought she was practically catatonic and you're telling me she was ignoring me on purpose," I said.

"Yep," Manuel said with a bitter smile on his face.

"Oh my god," I said, feeling like I had been had. Feeling sorry for the old woman. And she was looking down on me, in her feeble state. There was no winning in this country for me.

"Ain't that some shit," I mumbled, under my breath this time.

15: Black to the Beginning

To travel, I must always move through fear, confront terror.
It helps to be able to link this individual experience to the
collective journeying of black people, to the Middle Passage.

—BELL HOOKS

Cádiz is an easy city to navigate for the wandering tourist. Instead of a map, all you have to do is follow the blue line painted on the ground, which wraps around the city, looping through the dark, narrow streets, leading you to the most important historic sites the city has to offer. Arm in arm Manuel and I followed the line, feeling like first-time visitors to Spain. In the summer of 2001, we decided it was high time we learn something about the city of Manuel's birth. I'd been to Spain over a dozen times now and had never spent a single day in the city of Cádiz.

We poked our heads into candy stores and cathedrals, university buildings built in the sixteenth century and bustling cafés serving the city's famous fried seafood delicacies. We eventually found ourselves in a unique gift shop showcasing beautiful handcrafted pottery and local artwork and paintings. The building was a treasure itself, because even though from the outside the three-hundred-year-old structure looked weathered and gloomy, the inside had been modernized, complete with a see-through glass floor. It had been designed that way, the storekeeper informed us, so customers could view the secret room in the basement where contraband had been hidden at some crucial point in history. One year later and I couldn't remember what that contraband item had been. Manuel didn't remember either when I asked him. So my devious and creative mind decided it had been slaves. Yeah, that was it. Spain had had its own version of an underground railroad and we had discovered it!

Before I had time to consider why I, a random American tourist, would be the only person to know about Spain's underground railroad, I was on a mission. Basically I was just looking for a free trip. Not even. I was just trying to get the trip I was on paid for by a travel magazine. It was the summer of 2002 and as usual we were spending the majority of it in Spain with Manuel's family. As new parents, Manuel and I were enjoying the lifestyle that included an extended family that helped with babysitting and a housekeeper who did most of the cooking. The only thing marring my summer was the knowledge that I'd be broke when we returned to the States since I wasn't generating any income. I'd quit *Entertainment Weekly* after Esai was born and was trying to make it as a freelance writer. Thanks to getting my first book published in 2001, I was getting offers to write for a variety of magazines, but over the summer I had hit a dry spell, the main reason being that I was more focused on relaxing in the south of Spain than on pitching stories to magazines back in the States.

"So you're sure you don't remember what that shopkeeper said they were hiding in that secret room?" I asked Manuel again. We were lying on our bed during siesta time. Manuel was trying to sleep. I was trying to work this story idea out. "Could it have been slaves?" I probed.

"Sure, maybe. I don't know, Lori," Manuel said. When he called me Lori, instead of Titi, I knew he wanted me to shut up. But I couldn't. Not yet.

"Have you ever heard of there being slavery in your country?" I asked him.

"Nope," he said.

"So then how could there have possibly been slaves hidden in that room in that store?" I asked, exasperated that he wasn't trying to work with me here.

"How should I know?" he shot back. "It was your idea in the first place."

"Okay," I said. I wouldn't ask him anything else. I'd just talk aloud and if he had anything to add he could. "When you think about it, since Spain was supplying all the ships for the slave traders and Cádiz is like a perfect stopping point between Africa and the New World, I bet you anything some slaves were dumped here."

"Sounds possible," Manuel mumbled into his pillow. He was almost asleep.

I couldn't believe that I was about to hit on something groundbreaking and Manuel could drift off to dreamland. I tiptoed out of the room, careful not to wake my other baby, Esai, who was napping in his crib alongside our bed. I snuck out of the house and headed to the Internet café that was within walking distance from the house. It would be one of the few things open now because it catered to the tourists' schedule, not the Spaniards'. I was going to pitch a story idea via e-mail to an editor I had written for a few times at a new upscale travel magazine targeted to people of color.

On the walk over, I worked out the details in my head. As I thought about it, I did remember reading about that famous slave Olaudah Equiano who wrote in his autobiography about traveling in Spain, specifically in Málaga, and being treated far better than he had been in the States. Maybe he stuck around and lived in Spain for a while? Wasn't the movie Amistad about slaves and Spain? And even though I, Juan de Pareja was a novel, it was based on the true story of Velázquez's African slave. Clearly I was onto something. Just to cover my ass, though, as I wrote the pitch letter, I tried to sell the idea as kind of a quest story. I wanted to be the intrepid reporter who tries to track down any record of African slavery in Spain. I figured that way I'd be leaving a small window of opportunity to declare that I'd found nothing, but it could still be a good story following leads and incorporating a bit of history into a travel piece on the south of Spain, specifically Cádiz. By the time I hit Send on the computer I had convinced myself that there was indeed a story here waiting to be told. I still had more than three weeks left on my trip, and I figured if I got a response back right away, I would have plenty of time to do the research and write the story. I left the Internet café very pleased with myself and convinced I'd be a couple of thousand dollars richer by the time we made it home.

Apparently not. By the time we made it back to Brooklyn, I knew my story idea hadn't impressed the editors at *Odyssey Couleur* magazine. Not a single nibble on the pitch. And truth be told, with some time to think about it, I was happy they hadn't jumped on my enthusiastic e-mail, seeing as how I had been talking out of my ass, making up theories of slavery based on a desperate desire to find some part of myself in my husband's culture. Even though the summer had been a pleasant and relaxing one, every time I left the comfort of Manuel's home, I felt guarded and cynical when I walked the streets in the southern cities of Spain. People's eyes were always on me and my dark skin. Adults stared and children pointed. It was like Black was something they had never seen before. And it was true. Even I had never witnessed any aspect of Black culture or history reflected in Spain's art, music, or food. And the only other Black people I saw on a regular basis during my visits were African street vendors and the occasional tourist. Oh, and the one African woman who had opened a boutique in downtown Cádiz, where she was doing a brisk business selling African tchotchkes and braiding cornrows into Spanish teenagers' hair!

I yearned to find something that linked my history, my spirit, and my culture to Spain so I could feel genuine joy and excitement when we planned our annual excursions. So that I didn't feel so foreign in a country where I now had family. A country where I spoke the language and loved the cuisine. A country where we were considering buying a second home. But a country that at the end of the day had no place for me. I wasn't just a foreigner in Spain, like an Italian or a Greek. I was a stranger. An unknown. And that hurt me. A lot. And it hurt our marriage, too.

Manuel had agreed to live in America only if we could spend the summers in Spain. That would be enough to satisfy him, he said. I agreed initially when I still held romantic fantasies of Spain, but those had all been burned away with the Catholic Klansmen, the blackface mammies, Conguitos candies at every kiosk, and, even though they didn't mean to hurt me, Manuel's family in their absolute lack of knowledge about where I came from. Manuel thought I was being overly sensitive and maybe I was, but it had gotten to the point where I was making crazy suggestions like, "Instead of going to Spain, why don't we go to

Portugal and your family can visit us there?" Those inane suggestions just made Manuel angry and frustrated because of course he loved the culture that held no place for me. We fought about it and then we tried to ignore it. But the feelings never went away.

And then in September, when I had put slaves and Spain out of my mind, I got an e-mail. The editor at *Odyssey Couleur* was indeed intrigued but hadn't been able to respond until now. Was I still interested in doing the story? he wanted to know. Of course I was interested, but did he know I was no longer in Spain and doing the story would require that I return? I wrote him back expecting him to turn me down with an excuse that a new magazine never has enough money to send a writer abroad for a story. But he gave me the go-ahead and an expense account to boot! I experienced a moment of panic, wondering what would happen if I didn't find anything about Africans in the south of Spain. I pushed that worry aside and I said yes to the story and I signed the contract. I knew it was a strange request, but that night I prayed that my people had been enslaved at some point in Spain, just so that I could write this article and not be made to look a fool.

On the plane ride back to Spain, I reviewed my notes. I couldn't believe what I had found without even leaving the borders of New York City. At the Schomburg Center for Research in Black Culture, a reference library in Harlem that houses an extraordinary collection of the history of African people and their diaspora around the world, I discovered the truth. Not only did Cádiz serve as loading dock and transfer point for slaves, it was also the final destination for many of them. The books were all written in Spanish, so I didn't get all of the details straight, but it was clear that Spain had a long history of African slavery in her southern cities. In all of my visits and trips to Spain, I had never heard or seen any evidence of African slaves, and yet as I paged through the books scattered across the table in front of me with titles like *Esclavitud en Andalucía* and *La Compañía Gaditana de Negros* and *Los esclavos de Sevilla,* I came face-to-face with Spain's slaving past. But why wasn't it in the history books? I wondered. Why didn't people talk about it? Why did the average Spaniard have no knowledge of her own black history? I found one theory in a book by a professor at the university in Cádiz. In his book, he accused the Spanish government and the Catholic Church of deliberately erasing Spain's slaving past from their official history. I couldn't believe what I was reading. I wondered if I was misunderstanding the words, so I photocopied everything I could and planned to have Manuel translate it all for me. I was at once repulsed and ecstatic at finding this information. Now I knew that when I got to Spain, I'd have something real to investigate. A real mystery to solve.

When I was little, like between the ages of five and seven, I went through a serious detective phase. I dressed up as Sherlock Holmes for Halloween two years in a row. I begged my parents to buy me a detective kit so I could practice my sleuthing techniques. They indulged my whims, bought me the kit, and then regretted it immensely when they found white talc and black ink from my obsessive fingerprint dusting all over the house. Once I stopped pretending to be a detective, I started reading about super child sleuths like Encyclopedia Brown and Harriet the Spy. I began to carry around a notebook everywhere I went so I could record people's conversations and incriminating clues wherever I might find them. I never solved any one great mystery, but I never lost the taste for discovery. And now here I was, almost thirty years later, on a real adventure trying to discover Spain's hidden history and maybe a little piece of myself. Da-da-da dum!

To make sure I kept my feelings from getting hurt and to avoid getting too emotional over what could be a mind-blowing experience, I promised myself to keep the research professional. "Remember, Lori," I prepped myself as the plane was getting ready to land, "you are a journalist here on assignment. Leave no stone unturned and get the best story you can because this is business, not pleasure."

According to my notes from the Schomburg Library, Alfonso Franco Silva was the grandfather of the movement to bring Spain's hidden history to light. In his books he deemed it of the utmost importance that the truth of Spain's slaving history be revealed. His first book on the topic, *La esclavitud en Sevilla y su tierra a fines de la Edad Media,* had been published almost two decades earlier, but his argument about telling the truth still rang true today. I was ecstatic to discover after a brief Internet search that he still taught at the University of Cádiz and would be available to speak to me for my story.

I was so excited to meet Professor Silva, I arrived at the University of Cádiz twenty minutes early. I located his office, just to be safe, and then wandered around the university, wasting time. Even when Manuel and I had played tourist in Cádiz, we'd never made it here. Sitting up high and away from the bustle of the center of the city, the campus felt like a suburb of Cádiz. Palm trees and colorful flowers flanked the walkways between buildings. Bicycles and buses were the main sources of transportation for the students who meandered from class to class. Even in early November the weather was pleasant enough to wear short sleeves and a light sweater. I imagined Manuel, Esai, and me living here among the academics, Manuel teaching, me writing, and Esai playing with his little Spanish friends.

I hit Pause on my daydream reel and checked the time. I needed to head back to Professor Silva's office. As I neared his office, I started to get nervous. Would he be expecting a White American journalist? Would he be comfortable talking to a Black woman about slavery? And most important, was my Spanish good enough so that I'd sound like a competent professional and not a stuttering schoolgirl? Before arriving, I had taken the time to carefully write out my questions and asked Manuel's sister to proofread them for me. I also carried my tape recorder with me so I could review everything Professor Silva said with the comfort of Pause and Rewind buttons back at home.

Unfortunately, all of my preparation and anticipation landed very little new information. Franco Silva, it turned out, was a comfortable academic who genuinely wanted to tell me something of interest about Cádiz's connection to the slave trade but couldn't do much more than confirm that indeed there had been slaves in Cádiz and throughout Andalucía. "Spain was truly instrumental in introducing slavery to the Western world," he said. But when I asked him specific questions about Cádiz, he looked at me with sad eyes and said, "I'm not even really from here, so I can't tell you too much." Since 1977, when the book was published, he'd changed his focus from slavery to medieval studies. But you wrote the book on slavery in Andalucía, I wanted to remind him. And when I did try to get him to tell me more, he claimed he really didn't remember many specific details about the slavery issue. He couldn't come up with any numbers or statistics. He had no idea where I should look for any proof of the existence of Black slaves in Cádiz. Before I left his office, despondent and disappointed, he managed to compliment me on my accent and how well I spoke. That made me feel better and gave me the courage to ask if he had any ideas of whom I might talk to for some more information. And he gave me two names, Pedro Parrilla Ortiz and Isidoro Moreno.

On the bus ride back to Manuel's family's house, I had to give myself a pep talk. "Remember, Lori, no detective solves the crime on her first excursion out. Indiana Jones didn't find the Holy Grail on day one. And the Da Vinci code wasn't cracked with one interview." I listened to my inner Sherlock and then tried to imagine the reception I was going to get from my in-laws. Manuel's entire family, while maintaining an encouraging attitude about my work, swore up and down that they had never, ever, ever heard of Spain having slaves, unless you were talking prisoners of war back in the eighth century when the country was fighting its Moorish colonizers. But Black Africans? They were politely skeptical. As I expected, when I got home and told them about my meeting with Professor Silva, they made the right noises of sympathy and disappointment, but I know they were thinking, "Duh, what'd you expect? Kunta Kinte on a platter?" Well, the next day I was hopping a train and heading to the University of Seville, where I would meet with Isidoro Moreno. I prayed he'd be able to give me some answers.

I had an hour to kill when I arrived in Seville. The Andalusian capital is a sprawling metropolis famous for its hundred-plus-degree heat in the summer. But it rained the entire time I was there on that November day. Was the rain an omen warning me about what I was about to uncover? I wondered. I jumped in a taxi in front of the train station and went straight to the university. I decided to get something to eat while I was waiting, since I'd missed lunch. The area around the university was bustling with cafés, magazine kiosks, and bars. I didn't have to look far to find a restaurant. Right across the street I saw a pizza parlor and next door to that what looked like a hamburger joint. I crossed the street thinking about what I'd prefer to eat, Spanish pizza (might involve tuna) or a Spanish hamburger (might be served on Wonder Bread). In the end, my decision had nothing to do with food. I chose the *hamburguesería* because right in the doorway stood a statue of a fat Black chef, beckoning folks in. In the United States, this chef would have been considered classic negrobilia. In Spain, I didn't know what he was supposed to be. Maybe the equivalent of a lawn jockey? Last year, if I had seen this chunky Uncle Ben statue, I probably would have been offended and walked away from the restaurant. Now, with my newfound knowledge, I was intrigued and went into the shop, thinking perhaps the little man held a clue to Spain's Black past. Turns out he was just a handy sign to hold up the day's menu, but I still took his presence as a clue in this historical mystery. Signs of Blackness were everywhere, I was beginning to realize.

The university building that houses the anthropology and history departments in Seville used to be the city's tobacco factory. It looks like a castle on the outside. Inside it's a labyrinth of cavernous hallways, each one seeming to lead to yet another outdoor plaza with an ornate water fountain. I got lost twice following the directions of the concierge who had given me a laundry list of turns to get to Professor Moreno's office. The hallways were full of students, both Spanish and Americans enjoying their junior year abroad. I smiled as memories of Salamanca came rushing back. Finally in front of Professor Moreno's office, I pushed down the butterflies in my stomach and knocked on the door. "*Entra*," I heard. When I pushed the door open I saw two men, one White, one Black, seated at a table. The White man turned to me and said, "*Un momento.*" I nodded my head and went back into the hallway to wait. In about exactly *un momento*, the two men came to the door, finishing their conversation as they walked. They shook hands and the Black man, who was speaking Spanish with what sounded like a Dutch or German accent, smiled at me before he turned and walked down the hallway. Professor Moreno, a short, portly man with dark brown hair and a beard liberally streaked with gray, turned to me and ushered me into his enormous office. As we made our way to his desk I took in the African masks and native artwork carelessly scattered about. I was in the right place. I knew this man would give me the information I needed.

"So," he began, seated in his chair again, "how can I help you?"

I explained my official mission as a journalist writing a story about southern Spain's role in the slave trade. I didn't mention my own personal reasons for wanting to know the truth.

I clicked on my tape recorder as Professor Moreno began speaking. "Slavery is our dirty little secret," he started. "Up until the nineteenth century you could still find people who were descendants of African slaves in the small towns along the Atlantic coast like Gibraleón and Niebla. My own last name, Moreno, probably makes me a descendant of someone Black." I had to chuckle at that tidbit of information, seeing as how this man had milky white skin and stick-straight hair. If he carried Black blood in his veins, it was very well hidden. Still, I sat glued to my seat, forgetting to take notes, just trying to absorb the magnitude of what this man was telling me. This would be the point in the story where Sherlock says, "Elementary, my dear Watson." I'd found a portal to Spain's hidden history.

By the time I left Professor Moreno's office and stepped back out into the chilly rain, I felt like I was in a new country. Everything felt different. Spanish history had a totally new hue. I looked at the students milling around me and wondered if we might share a distant ancestor. The largest group of Andalucía's Black slaves came from Guinea and from the Wolof and Mandingo cultures, just like in the Americas. This was unbelievable. Perhaps a common ancestor had walked this land. Toiled in servitude, just like in the States.

"There was a big difference between the domestic slaves and those who worked in the mines, for example," Professor Moreno had explained when I asked him what life for the slaves in Spain was like. "In the mercury mines there were horrible conditions and a very high mortality rate. Those slaves who toiled in agricultural work in comparison to the domestic slaves also had a worse time." I thought about Manuel. We had always joked that he was really a Negro in disguise for all of our shared cultural habits. His love of pork, basketball, a long nap after a good meal. But now, I realized it really might be true. There was a good chance that my husband might have a Black African in his not so distant past. That might explain why our son had such a beautiful brown coloring even though Manuel is really pale. Applying that heinous one-drop rule from my own country, Manuel just might qualify to play on the dark side. The odds were in his favor. According to Professor Moreno, Blacks, both slave and free, at one time made up more than 15 percent of Seville's population. He thought those percentages were similar for Cádiz, and in fact at an even later date in Cádiz because southern Spain's power center shifted from Seville to Cádiz in the seventeenth century.

During the interview, I remembered a book Manuel had read for one of his graduate classes that claimed the Spaniards in Cuba treated their slaves better than the English. I asked Professor Moreno if there was any way to know how the Black Africans were treated in Spain, if they were abused mentally and physically like they had been in the States, if they were thought of as subhuman. Professor Moreno took off his glasses then and rubbed his eyes as he tried to give me the proper answer. "Slavery is slavery," he said. "I cannot compare the system in the United States to that in Spain. I can tell you, though, that here in Seville the Blacks were not hated, they were pitied. They were thought of as childlike and in need of guidance and direction. That's why they were referred to in the diminutive as 'negritos.' It wasn't until their numbers in Seville increased to almost fifteen percent of the population that more overt hostility toward Blacks was expressed." I pressed the professor for more details, because from his explanations of slaves being domestic servants and even artisans, helping skilled tradesmen, and even the existence of Black neighborhoods for free Blacks, slavery in Spain sounded much closer to indentured servitude than what I knew of slavery in my own country. I tried to explain to Professor Moreno how dehumanizing and cruel slavery had been in the United States and asked again if he thought the Spaniards were less cruel to their slaves. "Cruelty we know much of," he sighed. "For example, the slaves were branded on the cheeks upon their arrival here with this symbol." He grabbed a stray piece of paper on his desk, scribbled the letter *S* and what looked like a nail, and turned the paper to me. I didn't get it. "What is it?" I asked.

"It is the letter *S* and a nail," he answered. And then I got it. It was a play on words. The word for nail in Spanish is *"clavo."* Put an *S* in front and you have the word for slave: *"esclavo."*

As I walked through the darkening streets of Seville, I tried to imagine a time when thousands of Black people called this city home. When seeing a Black person speaking Spanish wouldn't cause a person to double back and look twice. Apparently Seville had such a numerous Black population (more than fifteen thousand documented in 1565), the city was known as "the chessboard." Of course I wouldn't have seen the slaves wandering freely at night because an ordinance was passed in the middle of the sixteenth century that after dark, all Blacks had to leave the city limits, meaning they had to exit the city walls that protected Seville from invasion. Today, Triana is an affluent suburb right outside the city center. Three hundred years ago it was where the Black people were banished to at night. Professor Moreno discouraged me from heading to Triana looking for some remnant of their presence. Nothing remained, he insisted. Instead he sent me to find a small church right in the center of the city called la Capilla de los Negritos. "That's where you'll find what you're looking for," Professor Moreno offered.

I found the church after passing by it twice, since it was sandwiched between a shoe store and a cell phone shop. Not exactly what I was expecting. There was no obvious sign on the door, but upon entering I knew I was in the right place. My eyes were immediately drawn to the life-size statue of the Virgin Mary behind the altar. She had two porcelain cherubs at her feet. One cherub was White, the other Black. More Black cherubs with fluffy little Afros were painted into celestial eternity on the ceiling, holding a ribbon that read "Reina de los Angeles." As I walked around the cozy interior of the tiny church, I noticed a plaque on the floor close to the altar. Although the words were scuffed, I could make out that I was standing on the tomb of Brother Salvador de la Cruz, *"El Negro de la Casa.* Baptized in March

1729." His burial date was illegible. I wondered if he was some official in the church. Professor Moreno had explained that the slaves had their own confraternities or religious brotherhoods, which was one of the only ways they could exercise some control over their lives. They could gather freely in the church and participate in the same holy day festivals as the Spaniards and conduct their business with some autonomy. They therefore had leadership roles within the confraternities, so maybe Brother Salvador was one of the church leaders.

On one side of the church I found a small statue of someone who I assumed was a Black saint. He had dark skin, wore a gold-tinged robe, and carried a heart and a cross in his hands. At his feet were two ceramic pots with fresh flowers. The white and blue pots both read *"Hmdad de los Negritos"* (Brotherhood of the Blacks). The plaque under the statue read "San Benito de Palermo." Apparently he was the patron saint of this brotherhood. I almost wept with emotion, realizing that the slaves' existence in Seville had been preserved. My people had stood in this church, sung here, and worshiped here. They had gathered and relaxed here, perhaps baptized their children and gotten married here. It was here that they expressed their humanity. I stood very still, considered lying down on the floor to rest my cheek upon the tomb of Brother Salvador, but simply closed my eyes instead and tried to connect with the spirits of *los negritos*. I sat down in a pew near the front of the empty church and marveled at this piece of history that stood unheralded by the citizens of Seville. How was it possible, I wondered, that when I asked some random people on the street why this church was called the "Chapel of the Little Black People," they had no idea. Some guessed it was because the church does charity work with African refugees (the newest *negritos* to come to Spain). A pharmacist at a nearby drugstore tried to make up an adequate reason referencing a period of history a long time ago, but came up short of any real reason. So even with the smiling Black cherubs blessing church visitors from the ceilings and *el negro de la casa* resting under the marble floor, the Spaniards remained ignorant of their own African past.

In 1649 a mysterious plague killed off one third of Seville's population. Being the poorest of the poor, the Black population in Seville was practically decimated and never regained its numbers. The Casa de Contratación, the official arm that regulated slaves coming from Africa and heading to the New World, moved from Seville to Cádiz and the slave route between Seville and Portugal was no more. Now, all of the slave ships coming from Africa were required to stop in Cádiz. And that's where I was heading next.

Before I started stalking the slave trade in Spain, the only way I'd heard Cádiz described was that many years ago it had a very open policy toward homosexuals and that it was one of the oldest cities in Europe. I knew the modern city had always relied on shipbuilding for its wealth, and when the shipbuilding industry went bust in the 1970s, the city experienced a devastating depression. From my perspective, it looked like it had never recovered. Cádiz always seemed like one of those places that had once been great and was now decomposing like an old forgotten corpse. At night when the peeling paint and dirty narrow streets are camouflaged in the shadows, sometimes you can imagine the city in its former state, but as soon as the sun rises again, the truth of its decay is revealed.

In the eighteenth century things were totally different for this little island city. Cádiz was becoming a superpower. Merchants from all over the world flocked to Cádiz to get in on the action. Money was flowing in from the Americas and the islands at a rate so fast, the citizens didn't know how to spend it all. Even the middle class reaped the benefits of the city's new wealth, and the preferred symbol of status was to own a slave. "Slavery in Cádiz was mostly domestic servitude," explained Pedro Parrilla Ortiz, the other historian Franco Silva had suggested I find. And I'm so glad I did.

Pedro's doctoral dissertation, *La esclavitud en Cádiz durante el siglo XVIII*, had become my new bible. I knew he'd have the answers to all of my questions, so I couldn't wait to talk to him. We met at a small café in front of la Plaza de las Flores in downtown Cádiz. Pedro had lived in Cádiz his whole life and now that he was approaching retirement age, he was tickled pink that an American journalist was actually here to pump him for information that he'd been carrying around for years. His thick Andalusian accent and propensity to tell ribald jokes made it difficult for me to understand him at first, but I dug in my heels and made the effort.

"There was no land to be worked in Cádiz," Pedro explained. "So most slaves functioned as maids or nannies or drivers." Pedro painted a rosier version of Spanish slavery than Isidoro Moreno had. "Many slaves lived in the best neighborhoods in the city with their owners," Pedro said. "They were perfectly integrated into society." In Cádiz, he explained, due to its small size, the people had to be okay with living in close quarters with Black people because, unlike in Seville, there really wasn't a place to isolate them. "Everybody got along because they had to. Just like in New York City," he laughed. What's more, Pedro confirmed, there was a lot of mixing between the races. "We Spanish, especially in the south, are a mixed people," he said solemnly. "And that's why we haven't been as racist or as cruel as the Anglo-Saxons." I wanted to believe Pedro. I wanted to believe that my husband's people and my new home away from home had a tradition of tolerance and understanding and diversity. This egalitarian version of history sounded so great, but I just couldn't figure out how tolerance, diversity, and slavery fit in the same sentence.

Once I'd finished my *zumo natural* and Pedro had downed his tonic water, we left the café and began our tour of Black Cádiz. Just like in Seville, the Black slaves and free Blacks had created their own confraternities. They were allowed to gather in churches outside the city limits, but as Cádiz continued to grow and expand, the Blacks were bounced from church to church, farther and farther away from the city center. The first church where the Confraternity of Rosario, the Black confraternity in Cádiz, gathered was the enormous boxy cathedral called la Iglesia de Santo Domingo. Sitting at the top of the city overlooking the port, it was probably one of the first buildings the Africans saw when they were hauled from the slave ships through an alleyway (now immortalized as the Callejon de los Negros) and sold in the slave market just below the cathedral steps. Nothing remains of the black occupation of the church, as they were evicted from the space when the area around the church became a sought-after neighborhood for Cádiz's wealthy citizens.

At 7:00 p.m., the doors to la Iglesia de Santo Domingo were wide open and a warm yellow light spilled out into the night. Pedro ushered me inside and explained some of the church's history, including a horrible fire that had destroyed many of the original artifacts and relics of the church. The building was awe-inspiring. Walking around the perimeter of the sanctuary, trying to be quietly respectful of the handful of people praying in the pews, I tried to imagine Black Africans here. I didn't have to imagine much because as I approached the doorway I saw a life-size statue of a brown Jesus.

"Is this from the time when the slaves were here?" I asked Pedro.

"No, no," he chuckled. "Everything was destroyed in the fire."

"Then why is this Jesus Black?" I queried.

"What do you mean?" he asked, looking truly puzzled.

I turned to the Jesus statue that stood not three feet in front of us.

"Um, this Jesus is Black, or at the very least he's a healthy brown. Why is that?"

"He's not Black," Pedro said, as if I had suggested the Holy Messiah was purple.

Just then a priest came over to us and he and Pedro greeted each other warmly. Pedro introduced me as the "American journalist," and then relayed to him my preposterous idea that this Jesus statue was Black or even Brown.

"No, he's not," the priest informed me as if I had asked a question.

Okay. Right. Whatever, I thought to myself. I just smiled at the two possibly color-blind men and decided to leave the not-Black Jesus alone.

Pedro then led me to the next church the slaves were allowed to use. We had to walk across half the *casco urbano* to get there. I would never have found la Iglesia Nuestra Señora del Rosario on my own. Like la Capilla de los Negritos in Seville, the baroque-style church sat humbly on a side street, alongside an apartment building and across the street from an upscale housewares shop. When we entered the small church my first thought was "cheesy." The space was so small that all of the religious statues and plastic flowers reminded me of the Indian restaurants in the East Village in New York City. Three hundred and sixty-five days a year they're dressed up with Christmas lights and shiny baubles. This church felt the same. I loved it! I tried to observe the space quietly as a few souls were praying, but I couldn't contain a squeal of joy as Pedro pointed out the marble altar toward the back of the church with the Virgin Mary flanked by two Black saints. One man and one woman. A small sign under the female saint's feet read "*El Altar de los Negros.*" This was the Black slaves' altar and it was still on display today. The male saint was an Italian named San Benito de Palermo and the female, according to her plaque, was Santa Efigenia, nun and princess of Ethiopia. I couldn't keep my smile to myself, and Pedro got caught up in my enthusiasm. We waited until we had exited the building to talk about it, though. "That was so amazing," I said to Pedro as we started walking. "I can't believe that altar still exists. And people here still don't know that there were slaves here? Unbelievable!"

As the night drew near and the sky grew dark, Pedro led me to a gorgeous public square called la Plaza de Mina, which he believed was once a slave market. Although the Spaniards never gained international fame from selling slaves, there were a few wealthy slave traders in Cádiz. Many of them were from northern Europe. Pedro speculated that the beautiful lime green mansion in one corner of the plaza was the company headquarters of one of the city's most successful slave traders. The company's insignia, a snake coiled around a flower, still sits above the door of what is now a government building. The beautiful flowers and enormous ancient Chinese palm trees surrounding the plaza and the fountain that reminded me of the Greek isles belied the history of the place. The beauty mocks its wicked history. I wondered if three hundred years ago when the Africans stood in the shade of these same palm trees, waiting to be sold to the highest bidder, they found this plaza beautiful, too.

"You know what's really interesting about the slave traders?" Pedro said to me as we headed back toward the center of the city.

"Hmmm," I murmured, lost in thought.

"Well, when the slave trade was abolished, these guys, many of them were English and Irish, took their money and invested it in another business. Guess what business it was?"

"What?" I asked, now paying more attention.

"Sherry," he said, laughing. "A lot of these great family sherry com-

panies in Jerez were slave traders. That's how we got the sherry industry down here." He laughed again.

"Really?" I asked.

"It's not in the history books," Pedro admitted, "but I believe it's true."

"From slaves to sherry," I said. "Hey, that'd make a great documentary film."

"Yeah, but I don't think those *dueños* want people to know if they
come from a slaving past," Pedro said chuckling.

"Probably not," I agreed.

Our final stop on this emotional tour was to visit the archives of the
Catholic Church in Cádiz. There were records there dating back to the
seventeenth century. "Whatever you want to say about the church,"
Pedro joked, "you gotta give them credit for keeping good records."
I expected the archives to be housed in the basement of the famed
catedral, but instead we entered a very modern building with an elevator that took us up to an air-conditioned library of history. I couldn't
believe my eyes when I saw the neatly catalogued stacks of oversized,
tattered brown books, bound with scarlet ribbons. Each book represented one calendar year and held the record of every *gaditano* born,
baptized, married, and dead—including the slaves.

Not that I hadn't believed these professors' tales, but considering
the lack of public knowledge on the subject, part of me was still a
little skeptical that so many Black Africans had lived in Spain. But
here was definitive proof. A careful hand had recorded "Ana, slave of
Antonio, born May 27, 1603." Or "*Antonia y Francisco, Negros,* married in 1602." Sometimes the slaves were recorded simply as "slaves
of" instead of given a last name. As time went on the label morphed
from "slave," to "*negro,*" to "*moreno.*" For a small time in history, Black
people in Spain were referred to and referenced as "*loros,*" which is a
parrot. The staff archivist didn't know why, but the term "*loro*" is still
considered a derogatory term for African people today in Spain.

I lovingly caressed the tissue-thin pages with the elaborate hand-
writing, trying to feel a connection to the past. I felt like I'd found the
hidden treasure. Nobody could deny this. This was the Holy Grail.
The undeniable proof that there had been Black people, both slaves

and free, populating the land of my husband's people. And not only that, but they had names, and husbands and wives and godparents! A godparent witnessed most slave marriages, interestingly enough. And their births and deaths and baptisms were recorded for the entire world to see and recognize. The only problem was of course that the world didn't know they should be looking.

My whole vision of Spain had to be altered or shifted or reconfigured somehow. According to Professor Moreno, even flamenco music, that uniquely Spanish music of lament and longing, probably carries with it the history of Black people. "It hasn't been officially proven by an eth-nomusicologist," Moreno said, "but some of the beats and rhythms of flamenco seem to have an African influence, which would make sense because of the Africans' time here and the birth of flamenco."

My mind was reeling with all of this new information. I felt as if my quest were almost over but there was still a crucial piece of this puzzle missing. What had happened to all the Black people? Did they just disappear? Professor Moreno's explanation just didn't seem pos-sible. He claimed the Blacks merged into the general population; the verb in Spanish was *blanquear*. They literally "whitened" themselves into nonexistence. Others went with their masters to the Americas. Pedro pretty much agreed with Professor Moreno's explanation, say-ing that the Black Africans simply mixed with the general population until they were no more. Many of them left Cádiz, when slavery was abolished in 1830, to go work in the countryside, where there was more work. There, Pedro claimed, they melted into the Spanish land-scape. Although, Pedro added, he did see certain negroid features in the people of Andalucía, even if they did have pale white skin.

"My wife has Negro features," Pedro boasted. "And her last name is *Morillo*." Translation: little Moorish man.

I now knew I had plenty of information for my article. On the bus ride back to my in-laws' house I went over my notes and looked around at my fellow bus passengers. We're not so different, I thought to myself. They just don't know it because the Spanish government deliberately covered up their Black past in an attempt to alter their historical reputa-tion. I guess liar is better than slave owner in some people's eyes.

✿ 16: Kinky Gazpacho

I didn't know Spain had a Black history when I was child. But maybe that's why Spain was calling me to her, to tell her truth. It's so strange because Spanish people do not recognize Black as something familiar. But there is something about the Spanish soul, perhaps its own Black past, that welcomes Black people into the country. Historically, at least, this has been true. During the Spanish Civil War, Black American men and women, feeling compelled to aid the Spanish in their fight against fascism, flocked to Spain and received a hero's welcome. "Spanish women showered the Black men with smiles and flowers," recalled a White American volunteer from Detroit. Indeed, after the segregated America they left behind, the Black volunteers who came to Spain tasted their first bit of humanity. "I never felt more like a man than in Spain," said Luchelle McDaniels, an African-American soldier who fought in the famous integrated Abraham Lincoln Brigade.

Before and after the Spanish Civil War, Black writers like Langston Hughes, Nella Larsen, and Richard Wright all found solace and serenity in Spain. Chester Himes, the father of Black-American crime writing, made the south of Spain his home during the last fifteen years of his life, having fled America's crippling preoccupation with race in the 1950s. Himes found the small fishing village of Moraira infinitely more humane than his life in southern California and even Paris, where he lived for a time. And yet I never knew of these Black writers and artists fleeing to Spain while I was planning my own escape.

We were on our way back. Not since the summer before my junior year of college had I been this excited to get to Spain. Like then, this time I was going for me, to discover something about myself. Officially, we were visiting Manuel's family for spring break, but I was determined to continue on with my quest. I felt like I'd wasted so many years being resentful and wishing I were anywhere else besides Spain that I never saw the truth. I missed the evidence all around me. I ignored the clues and the signs in front of my face. Now, Spain's black blood seemed to seep through the cracks on the sidewalk and I could finally see it with unbiased eyes.

And this time, Manuel was coming with me. He seemed to be just as excited as I was about my discoveries. "I just can't believe all this stuff you're finding," he kept saying. "I can't believe they never taught us any of this in school." Manuel vowed that the great cover-up about Spain's history would stop with him. He would make sure his students learned the truth about Spain.

Manuel was now a teacher at a private high school in Philadelphia, where we had moved after the birth of Addai, our second son. New York had proved to be too costly for us to stay. We tried to justify living in a one-bedroom, overpriced apartment in a fourteen-story high-rise, using the diversity factor as reason number one to make a go of it. Our precious SpaNegro boys never stood out among the JapaNegros, the chocolate-vanilla swirls, and the rest of the motley crew of multi-culti kids on the playground. And in the cocoon of brownstone Brooklyn and the hectic streets of Manhattan, nobody cared that Manuel was my (pale) partner of choice. But we just couldn't commit to that lifestyle. Our boys demanded room to grow and I just got too tired taking two buses and a subway to go grocery shopping. We chose Philly because it was close enough to New York that I could continue to work in the publishing industry and because we found a little enclave in Philadelphia called Mount Airy that professed to be the most integrated neighborhood in America. We felt right at home as soon as we moved in. There wasn't nearly as much United Colors of Benetton–style diversity, but people didn't stare at our blended little family, either.

As soon as we got off the airplane in Seville, I tried to look at things differently. I sniffed the air for a whiff of familiarity. I tried to hear new sounds. Of course I didn't. I was trying a little too hard. The fact of the matter was, even though I had discovered Spain's hidden past, it didn't mean any Spaniard was aware of it. In fact, when we arrived, Spain was embroiled in a racial quagmire of its own making. The influx of Black African soccer players on Spanish *fútbol* teams had gotten the locals peeved. It had become a common practice for fans to throw bananas on the fields and make monkey noises when the Africans played. I learned about this on my first night back, when the cameras panned the audience at a local soccer game Manuel's family was watching on TV. It seemed every other person in the stands carried a homemade poster that read "*Gaditanos Contra el Racismo.*" Citizens of Cádiz Are Against Racism.

"What's that about?" I wondered aloud. Nobody seemed to hear me and rather than push the issue I asked Manuel about it later that night as we were getting ready for bed. He told me what had been happening, ashamed once again of his people's actions. "But," he said in their own defense, "apparently the bananas and stuff have been happening more in the north. That's why the *gaditanos* are trying to make a point." He thought for a moment and then said, "I don't know if I'm full of shit or something, but I think southern Spaniards are less racist than northern Spaniards. I used to think it was because we've always been looked down on as the poor stupid ones who don't even speak properly in Spain. But now I wonder if it has something to do with the fact that we had slavery here."

"What are you saying?" I probed. "That somehow your history of slavery here in the south makes you more connected with Black people?" I asked.

"Well, yeah," he said. "I mean, it's just a theory, but I'd like to find out if it has any merit."

Manuel and I were in this together now. He wanted to prove that his Black past somehow influenced his current circumstances. I wanted to know what part of my culture could be found embedded in Spanish culture. Basically, I wanted to find where the Kinky intersected with the Gazpacho. We both wanted to know how it was possible that the people of Cádiz could remain so blissfully ignorant of their own Black history when the clues were all around them. We decided to take our questions to the street.

Taking our lead from bad reality ambush TV shows, Manuel and I stationed ourselves on the corner of the Callejón de los Negros. Pedro Parrilla Ortiz had already explained to me that the street was so named because it was the passageway the Africans were hauled through from the slave ships at the port into the city. Another historian told me it was the passage the Blacks used to haul cargo from the city to the port. Manuel and I decided to ask some locals about the origins of the street's name. Although it was a small street, it wasn't hidden and it intersected with a major thoroughfare. Sure, many people might not have cause to walk through el Callejón de los Negros, but the sign itself couldn't be missed.

So I stood aside with my map, trying to look like a tourist. Manuel would then approach people and ask them innocently, as if he didn't know, "Excuse me, why is this street called Callejón de los Negros?"

The first people he asked were some construction guys, working on a building directly across the street. They both shrugged their burly shoulders and said they had no idea. An older gentleman with thick glasses and a derby hat, overhearing Manuel's questions, said he might be able to help.

"You see," he began, "a long time ago when the Phoenicians and the Visigoths ruled Spain, there was a lot of fighting and wars." He then proceeded to detail several wars and the history of Cádiz from the Middle Ages. Finally Manuel had to interrupt. "So what does this have to do with the Callejón de los Negros?" he asked politely. The little old man looked at him square in the eyes and said, " I have no idea."

Soon a couple in smart navy blue business suits, looking like they were heading into the nearby Palacio de Congresos, came walking toward us. Manuel detained them, playing up his innocence act. "Excuse me," he said. "Do you know why this street is called Callejón de los Negros? We can't figure it out." Maybe because they were in suits and were used to giving people answers, they gave us this explanation. The man started with, "It must come back from the time when the Spanish were going to the Americas."

"Yes," the woman chimed in. "It was one of those popular names of the times," she said.

Then the man added for clarification, "Probably a lot of people walked through here, probably some Black people walked through here, too."

"So there's no other special meaning for the name," Manuel probed.

"No," they both answered.

"There's no special meaning," the man repeated.

"It was just a popular name at the time," the woman added.

"Muy interesante," I said.

Once they were out of earshot, Manuel and I looked at each other and burst out laughing. "Alley of the Blacks sounds like a really popular name," I repeated. It was hilarious, the earnestness with which people made this stuff up, but at the same time, it depressed me to think that Spaniards had no idea that African slavery existed in their country. Even when the clues and memories were as obvious as little Black angels floating around their churches.

"Let's ask one more person," Manuel urged. He was enjoying this little game. He stopped an older couple on their way home from the market. They both looked to be in their late sixties and still happily in love in that comfortable way of two people who've lived a life together. He carried the groceries and she had her arm looped through his. I hoped Manuel and I would be so content after forty years together.

"Perdone," Manuel began, and the two stopped to give us their attention. "Do you have any idea why this street is called Callejón de los Negros?" he asked. We both wondered what fresh spin this nice couple would offer us.

"Sí, sí," the man answered confidently. I got ready to keep my eyes from rolling.

"When the ships came to and from America and Africa, loaded with slaves, they would walk them through that street and keep them there," he said pointing to the Iglesia del Rosario, the church Pedro told me had been the slaves' first meeting place.

"Really?" Manuel said, playing the innocent, but equally surprised that we had finally found someone who knew the truth. "I didn't know we had slaves in Spain," Manuel said to the man.

And his wife answered then, looking directly at me. "Yes, we did. In Cádiz we've had all kinds of people." And then she said something that at first seemed like a non sequitur: "You see, in Cádiz we are not racist," as if by enslaving Africans that made *gaditanos* open-minded to diversity. She smiled at me when she said that, a smile that seemed to say "You are welcome here."

Her husband added then, "It's amazing because really it happened almost yesterday." Manuel thanked them and they went on their way, arm in arm.

"I wonder why they knew the truth and nobody else did," I said to Manuel. "We should have asked them. I mean, maybe it's not such a hidden history after all. Maybe the people who want to know do know."

After I took Manuel all around Cádiz and showed him everything that remained of Black life—retracing the route Pedro led me on the year before—he wanted to do more detective work of his own. One day we decided to hit all of the churches and cathedrals in Cádiz to see if we could find more proof that Black people had once lived here.

We left early in the morning, leaving both boys in the care of their Abuela Elisa, who had been kind enough to take two weeks off from work so Manuel and I could investigate "our roots." I loved that this historical fact-finding mission meant something to both of us now. It wasn't just my little project anymore. I still didn't get the idea that Manuel's family knew exactly what I was trying to find, but they were enthusiastic nonetheless that whatever I was doing was bringing us to Spain more frequently. They never probed too deeply about what I was finding, mostly confining their questions to "How'd it go today?" and "Are you finding what you need?" It was actually a relief that they didn't want many details because I wasn't prepared to have a real conversation about race with my Spanish family. I didn't really want to know if deep down they believed Black people were less intelligent and childlike. I didn't want to hear their opinions on Black female sexuality. I didn't want to hear them pontificate on the Black male athlete. So better to just keep smiling and answering "Fine."

Manuel parked the car in a modern underground parking structure, which always struck me as completely incongruous in a city that was nearly three thousand years old. We began our quest in a small church that lay in the shadows of one of the largest and most famous cathedrals in Cádiz. It was called la Iglesia de Santa Cruz.

It was springtime, so most *gaditanos* were preparing for Semana Santa. That meant that the inside of the church felt more like a mechanic's garage than a house of worship. Massive floats in various states of repair littered the sanctuary floor. The only people in the building when we arrived were a few guys with soldering irons putting some final touches on their Virgin Mary floats. Even with the power tools on full blast I felt like we should whisper out of respect.

Manuel and I walked around the perimeter of the church, looking at the statues and candles and ancient relics hanging on the walls. Here was a lock of hair of some saint; there were the rosary beads of another. I wandered over to another vestibule and had to bite my lip to keep from yelling aloud. I found a Black saint. I called Manuel over, barely able to contain my excitement. "Look," I said, pointing to the small statue. The plaque at his feet read "San Pedro Apostol." Unlike the Black saint in la Iglesia del Rosario, this saint was dark brown instead of tar black. He had long tapered fingers, a halo, and a golden robe. There were pennies around his feet. Pedro Parilla Ortiz never showed me this church or this saint. Was this another church where the slaves worshiped? Or did Spanish people just like to worship Black saints? Was Manuel right? Did southern Spaniards just feel comfortable with Blackness?

Manuel was impressed. "See, we have Black people all around us all the time," he said. As I was turning to walk back toward the door, scribbling notes in my notebook, Manuel tapped me on the shoulder. "Uh, Lori, you might want to look at this," he said. I turned around to see what he was looking at and I almost fell over. It was a giant, life-size Jesus, complete with a crown of thorns. He was wearing a blue velvet robe and fresh red carnations had been strewn across his bare brown feet. But the thing was, he was Black! He wasn't just a shade darker than the average Jesus: this son of God had dark brown skin and—the telltale sign of Negritude—thick, brown, kinky hair.

"Isn't that amazing," Manuel said. "I wonder who it is?" I looked at my husband, who still wanted to call himself a Catholic, and laughed.

"Uh, honey, that's Jesus," I said. "If the hairdo and the beard don't clue you in, the crown of thorns is a dead giveaway."

"But he's Black," Manuel said, revealing his own cultural bias. I realized at that moment that without stopping to edit his thoughts, the idea that Jesus could be a Black man was inconceivable to my European husband.

"Yeah, I noticed that," I said. "I can think of a lot of Black churches in America who'd love to get their hands on this beautiful statue, but I don't understand why your people want him in their church." I looked around the vestibule for a clue. Maybe he was on loan from Africa for the Semana Santa celebration? The only piece of information I found was a sign that said "Jesús de Medinacelli." We asked one of the guys on break from float duty who this Jesús de Medinacelli really was, but he just shrugged his shoulders and said he wasn't exactly sure. He did mention that he'd heard that he was a Jesus for the gypsies and that's why he was brown.

Okay, so the gypsies have their own Jesus. Interesting. I wondered if Chinese Christians have a Chinese Jesus. Why not? It makes him more personable, right?

Stepping out of the dark cathedral, Manuel and I were both lost in thought. How is it possible that after all of these years of coming to the south of Spain, I never noticed all of these signs of Blackness? And what did it mean that a culture that seemed overtly devoid of any kind of Black experience has something so deeply personal as Black religious icons all over the place? After a wee bit of research I discovered that Jesús de Medinacelli is a very popular icon throughout Spain, from Madrid all the way down to Algeciras. The original Jesús de Medinacelli statue sits in a church in Madrid. In the seventeenth century he was brought to Madrid, having been rescued from Morocco, where

he'd been held hostage by the Moors after the Spanish tried to conquer part of their land. He was given the name Medinacelli because
the duke of Medinacelli was the prime minister of Spain at the time
of the statue's arrival in Madrid. Today people push and shove to ride
behind the Jesús de Medinacelli float every Semana Santa because he
is supposed to bring good fortune to those who pray to him. So basically that means that the Black Jesus is the cool guy during Holy Week
in Spain. Go figure.

I was confused. With bananas covering the soccer fields in Spain,
I couldn't possibly say Spaniards weren't racist, but discovering all
of this history and iconography so meshed into the fabric of Spanish
culture, I still couldn't answer the simple question, Do Spaniards love
or hate Black people? I decided I needed to get a second opinion.

Pierre and Marie Etienne are American citizens, but they were both
born and raised in Haiti. They've lived all over the world but spent
more than thirty years in the United States. Now they live in Spain. In
the southern port city of Algeciras, to be exact. When it came time to
retire, this distinguished Black couple—he was a chemist, she a trans-
lator at the United Nations—decided they wouldn't be able to maintain
their quality of life in the northern suburbs of New York City. So they
packed up their lives and moved to Spain, where they've been living for
the past five years. I decided to go have lunch with them to see if they
could tell me if Spaniards loved or hated Black people. If anyone would
know, or at least have a good working theory, I figured it was them.

Pierre picked me up from the bus station in Algeciras. Dressed in
blue jeans, a blue pinstriped button-down shirt, and a gray sweater,
he immediately reminded me of my uncle Walter. Conservative but
relaxed. When we arrived at their apartment, his wife, Marie, took
one look at me and decided I reminded her of her younger daughter.
In dress, Marie was the opposite of her husband. She wore a casual
baby blue sweatsuit with capri pants and black ballet slippers. Whereas Pierre spoke only when he had something of import to say, Marie
chattered on in her delightful singsongy mixture of French, English,
and Spanish. I liked her immediately.

The Etiennes' four-bedroom apartment was decorated with a mix of Haitian art, family photos of their three children, and paintings and artwork of Marie's. Since moving to Spain, Marie had taken up painting and flamenco dancing, and she taught yoga at the community center. We sat down for lunch in the kitchen right away.

"So what did you want to talk about?" Marie asked me as I reached for more avocado salad.

"Well, I'm trying to figure out Spain's relationship with Blackness. Ever since I came here ten years ago, I've thought of this country as racist, even though the racism seemed to be based on ignorance and not a history of hatred like in the United States. But now I've discovered that Spain had a long history of African slavery."

Both Pierre and Marie seemed surprised by this. They didn't know that Spain had imported and utilized slaves.

"So what I'm trying to figure out is," I continued, "is Spain really racist or conversely, are Spaniards, specifically in the south, really comfortable with Black people because they've actually had Black people in their midst forever?" As I heard these words tumble out of my mouth, I wondered what these wonderful people could actually tell me. There was no real answer to this question. And one couple couldn't gauge the prejudice factor of an entire country's population. Pierre interrupted my musings.

"You know, these are good questions. We moved here because Marie's brothers live here, and so we were familiar with Spain and we have family here. But still we weren't one hundred percent sure what we were getting into." He laughed at the memory. Marie added, "Yes, all of our friends thought we were crazy."

Pierre continued, "But when we first got here, there was a lot of unemployment and there was a lot of anti-immigrant sentiment. A lot of Moroccans and Africans were feeling that. But because we were retired and not looking for work, we didn't experience the animosity. But I think if we had, we wouldn't be so happy."

Marie jumped in. "I love Spain and I have never felt any kind of racism. People here have embraced me. I teach yoga. I belong to a social club. I go to church. Maybe it is because my brother is a well-respected lawyer here in Algeciras and people know I am his sister, but personally I think here we do not encounter racism like it was in the United States."

I was dubious that in all their years coming here to visit and now after five years of living that they'd never been the targets of any racist treatment. But Marie insisted that they hadn't. "You know, really I don't feel the people here are racist. My brother is married to a Spanish woman and they have two daughters and the children are happy."

Pierre interrupted his wife. "Actually, didn't you say the older one had some problems?"

Marie pooh-poohed her husband's reminder, telling me that the girl had been teased about her hair while growing up. I wanted to say "aha!" but of course even in melting pot America little black girls get teased and tormented about their hair, so I couldn't consider that a Spanish thing. But talking about her nieces who were both now married to Spanish men brought back a memory for Marie.

"You know, now that I think about it, I do remember something from when our children were little. Whenever we would bring them to Spain, the people would always reach out to pat them on the head. I asked my brother about this because it bothered me. My brother said Spanish people believed it was good luck to touch a Black child."

"That's what I'm talking about," I said, slamming my hand on the table. "Stuff like that makes me think Spaniards have no clue about real Black people, but on the other hand, they seem comfortable with us."

"Yes, I don't think they have any problem with Black people," Marie reiterated.

"It's more the Moroccans whom they seem to disrespect," Pierre added.

"Yeah," I agreed. "One of Manuel's cousins told me in a rare moment of candid conversation that the racial pecking order in Spain would be Blacks on top because we're generally happy people, but South Americans and Gypsies are generally associated with delinquent behavior."

"But here in Algeciras," Marie clarified, "there are so many Moroccans coming in and out and the people here are so used to them. It's very diverse here."

I had to admit that while waiting for Pierre at the bus station, there were throngs of Moroccan women, decked out in their native djellabas, waiting in taxi lines with stuffed suitcases bigger than themselves. I expected the taxi drivers to be rude and angry, being forced to lift these gargantuan bags, but they were just as polite and friendly and laid back with the Moroccan women as they were with the Spaniards.

"As long as everyone has his or her job," Pierre summed up, "everybody's happy."

When I got back to Manuel's house, I was smiling. Lunch with Marie and Pierre had been great. It was really refreshing to hear from a Black couple who *loved* Spain. Marie even confessed that she wished she had raised her children in Spain, that's how much she appreciated the culture and values of her adopted homeland. "Every country is racist," she told me. "There is no magic place where racism does not exist. But here in Spain people tell you what they think to your face and it is over. It's not like in the United States, where people may be polite to your face but would stab you in the back because of the color of your skin."

I couldn't wait to tell Manuel how positive my lunch date had been. He'd be thrilled to hear a Black couple had given Spain the thumbs-up, especially for raising children, since he seriously wanted to spend a year or two living in Spain with our children. For the first time, I was feeling like that might be a good idea. Nothing had really changed in Spain. The people hadn't gone through collective racial awareness training, but I felt like I had. Spanish people for the most part didn't know their own history, but still it seemed to tumble out anyway, like any bones stashed away in a closet will. Just because they don't celebrate Black History Month doesn't make them incapable of embracing Black culture in other incarnations. Not to mention, there seemed to be a small movement growing in the academic community to expose Spain's hidden history. Isidoro Moreno had mentioned documentary films being made, conferences and conventions being organized, and research dollars being allocated to bring this history out into the open. So maybe one day there would be a Spanish Black History Month.

Everyone was in the kitchen when I got back to Manuel's parents' house from my lunch in Algeciras. As I walked to my room to drop off my purse, one of the pictures on the wall in the hallway caught my eye. The series of prints had hung here for years, but this was the first time I had stopped to really examine them. They were prints of Black people. Slaves, I presumed. In the sugarcane fields. Why did I never notice this before? My in-laws had real negrobilia. I had an aunt back in Milwaukee who'd pay good money to get her hands on these pictures. I wondered if it was really true that we only see what we want to see.

As I changed out of my visiting clothes into my comfy sweats and flip-flops, I couldn't help but marvel at this journey I'd been on since childhood. I shuffled into the kitchen feeling all karmic and happy. Manuel, his mother, and his sister were sitting around the table. My children, I was told, were at Tía Paqui's house. I plunked myself down and started nibbling on the olives in the middle of the table.

"So how'd it go?" Manuel asked.

"Great," I said, leaning over to kiss him on the cheek.

"Ay, my wife loves me," Manuel exclaimed. His mother smiled.

"Lori," Eli said, and I turned my attention to her. "We found something for you."

"What is it?" I asked, hoping it wasn't another well-meaning but ill-fitting article of clothing. Spanish clothes just never fit my Black American body.

"Mira," Eli said, whipping out a Black baby doll with warm brown skin and dark brown hair from under the table. The doll wore a white dress and had a blue ribbon in her hair.

"Where did you get that?" I asked.

"It was mine when I was a little girl," Manuel's mom said, smiling at me and her own memories.

"And now I have it," Eli chirped in. "It's always been in my room on the shelf with my other dolls."

I had never noticed a Black doll in my sister-in-law's room.

"Why did you have a Black baby doll?" I asked my mother-in-law.

"I don't know," Elisa answered, wrinkling her brow trying to remember. "I guess because she was the prettiest one. And I wanted the prettiest doll."

And just like that, tears welled up in my eyes. That simple explanation absolutely devoid of racial meaning flipped a switch in my brain. I jumped up and hugged my mother-in-law then.

"Gracias, Elisa," I said.

"For what?" she said, laughing at my high-jinks emotions.

For liberating me from my own anxiety, I wanted to say. For giving me the freedom to just be and to strip away all of the racial baggage I've hauled back and forth across the Atlantic Ocean all these years. For making me think about Spain in individual instances instead of broad strokes of condemnation. For opening my mind up to the possibility of Spain's redemption. But since I didn't know how to translate "racial baggage," I just said, "Because you think I'm pretty."

Manuel grabbed me then and kissed me hard on the mouth and said, *"Ay, mi niña."*

Epilogue

Of course there is no happily ever after in real life. But happily is how I go to Spain now and forevermore.

Acknowledgments

Two people, Quincy and Morris, created this life I just chronicled. I thank them profusely for not only bringing me into this world, but for sacrificing so much to make my time on this earth such a fantastic experience. They stayed grounded so I could spread my wings and fly. There are not enough words in the English language to express my gratitude to them.

And then there's Manuel, my biggest cheerleader, faithful first reader, eagle-eyed copy editor, best friend, and *media naranja*. Without him there would be no story, no gazpacho, no romance. My love affair with Spain would have died in 1992 and I would have never discovered Spain's colorful past.

Since this is a memoir, technically I feel I should thank every single person who passed through my life and made an impression on me, but that would be a really long list. So instead I will thank my entire family, both here in the States and my Spanish family in Andalucía, for their love and support of all of my creative endeavors. Even when they didn't really get what it was I was trying to accomplish, they have always treated me like a superstar when I needed it most.

Of course big ups must go to my agent, Marie Brown, who read at least a hundred versions of *Kinky Gazpacho* before I finally figured out what I really wanted to say. And she never gave up on me or suggested I seek therapy. She just kept an open mind and an open door. I thank her for believing in my ability to get the job done.

And to the people at Atria, especially Malaika and Krishan, thank you for not only buying this book, but for believing in it and loving it as much as I do.

And to Esai and Addai, it is because of you that I needed to document that when Black and Spanish come together, the results are beyond delicious. You two are forever my inspiration and my greatest joy.

Josephine Baker and Zora Neale Hurston, thank you for doing it better than I have and for giving me a model for my fantasies.

And finally to my Spanish teachers, the ones who sparked the flame, kept my dreams alive, and tried in vain to teach me the subjunctive verb forms: Sr. Betancourt, Profe (Jane Spector), Reyes Lázaro, and Daniel Pastor García. *Muchas gracias.*

About the Author

Lori L. Tharps is a freelance journalist, editor, author, and mom. Originally from Milwaukee, Wisconsin, she is a graduate of Smith College and Columbia University's Graduate School of Journalism. She lives in Philadelphia and spends a lot of time in Spain.